The Habit of Happiness

The Habit of *HAPPINESS*

Exploring the Beatitudes

by

Randal Earl Denny

Beacon Hill Press of Kansas City
Kansas City, Missouri

ISBN: 0-8341-0399-0

Printed in the United States of America

Dedication

To my father and mother
EARL AND THELMA DENNY
A home where I was loved and knew it;
where we shared the music of the Master;
where, following their footsteps,
I came to meet their Christ.

Contents

Foreword

If the Sermon on the Mount is the "Constitution" of the kingdom of God, the Beatitudes must comprise some of the most important "Articles" of that document.

Randal Denny discusses these vital precepts in a most engaging way in *The Habit of Happiness.* From the perspective of a pastor whose major responsibility is relating the life and teachings of Jesus to twentieth-century saints and sinners, he makes these "Blesseds" both practical and pertinent. No ivory tower abstractions these. They speak the language of our lives, lifting us to that higher spiritual ground which is the birthright privilege of every Christian.

I heartily recommend this delightful volume to the new convert, the seasoned disciple, and to all who find themselves between these extremes. Your mind will be enlightened and your heart enlarged as you come to a new understanding of these timeless truths. Read each chapter carefully. Then pause to prayerfully accept the insights which the Spirit will make relevant to your personal situation.

May you find a new dimension of depth in your Christian life and service as you develop "the habit of happiness."

—Eugene L. Stowe
General Superintendent,
Church of the Nazarene

Acknowledgments

Appreciation is hereby expressed for permission to quote from copyrighted materials as follows (see reference notes for bibliographical data):

Publishers-Hall Syndicate: Ann Landers' column in the *Modesto Bee.*

Abingdon Press: Myron S. Augsburger, *The Expanded Life.*

Hallmark Cards, Inc.: Peter Marshall, *New and Inspiring Messages.*

"Foundation for Christian Living": a sermon by Norman Vincent Peale.

Wm. B. Eerdmans Publishing Co.: D. Martyn Lloyd-Jones, *Studies in the Sermon on the Mount,* Vol. I.

Nazarene Publishing House: Aarlie J. Hull, "A Christian Woman's World," *Herald of Holiness,* March 14, 1973; W. E. McCumber, *Preaching Holiness from the Synoptic Gospels.*

Herald Press: John M. Drescher, *Now Is the Time to Love.*

Baker Book House: Charles W. Koller, *Sermons Preached Without Notes.*

Marshall, Morgan, and Scott: J. Sidlow Baxter, *A New Call to Holiness.*

Harper and Row Publishers: William Barclay, *The Beatitudes and the Lord's Prayer for Everyman.*

A word of appreciation to the loyal congregation of the First Church of the Nazarene in Modesto, Calif., is in order. It was a challenge to share God's Word with them during which time this book was written.

My personal indebtedness is to Kathleen Ogburn, a secretary *par excellence,* who labored with diligence and loyalty with the preparation of this manuscript. For her encouragement I owe a great debt.

—RANDAL EARL DENNY

1

The Beatitudes

Matthew 5:1-12

The Habit of Happiness

Ann Landers received a thought-provoking letter written by a recent visitor to the United States.

Dear Ann Landers:

For the past six months I have been a visitor in your wonderful country. Now that I am about to return to Austria, I would like to tell you my impressions of America.

Your country is indeed the most prosperous in the world. The spaciousness of America is overwhelming; the beauty, awesome. I love every inch of it.

But, Miss Landers, something is wrong with the people. They are friendly and helpful but they appear to be unhappy. In America there is much pleasure, but no joy. Americans seem always to surround themselves with so much noise. They even walk with radios in their hands.

Your people hurry a great deal. They are afraid of quiet—afraid to think. And as one listens to much of the social conversation, it is apparent that they do not think. They repeat only what they heard on the radio or television.

I had a wonderful visit. Your country is the most beautiful in the world. You have lofty mountains, great prairies, endless deserts, beautiful tropics, and imposing cities. May God bless all Americans and may you find the true joy that mere pleasure cannot bring.

—A Thankful Guest[1]

The heartache of this nation one can understand, but the Church of Jesus Christ ought to make a difference in the moral and spiritual climate. His Church has been entrusted with the happiest news the world could ever hope to hear. The Church has reason to rejoice in Christ. But somewhere in the shuffle, most Christians seem to have lost the habit of happiness.

Hardly a week goes by that a pastor is not forced to make apologies for professing Christians who are very unhappy people. Society is watching for a note of joy. A sad world cannot be sweetened by a sour religion. In spite of many sad caricatures, Christianity is basically a religion of joy. Christ was such a happy Person that He referred to himself as the Bridegroom of the world.

Jesus emphasized the habit of happiness as He began the Sermon on the Mount with a list of "Blesseds"—eight ways to be happy. His words were practical. He told men how to live, how to act towards God, how to act toward their fellowmen, and how to live with themselves. The Beatitudes are not for some far-off day when Christ returns. They are designed for living today.

The Sermon on the Mount, including the Beatitudes, is for the Christian, the believer in and follower of Jesus. The principles of godly living set forth are not intended for the unconverted. If every Christian would live by the Sermon on the Mount, people around him would know that the gospel is true, that it is dynamic and alive. They would not go looking for anything else.

The greatest deterrent to the unconverted onlooker is the Christian who has not formed the habit of happiness. Jesus set down the Beatitudes as descriptions of the character of His disciples. He is not suggesting, "Live like this and you will become a Christian." The Master is saying, "Because you are a Christian, live like this." The Beatitudes are how Christians ought to live, how they are intended to live—with the habit of happiness.

I

The Christian has the Potential for Happiness

Jesus was giving the Beatitudes to men who were already disciples. But obviously they were not yet living up to their potential.

Many well-meaning people expect that when Jesus comes into their lives, all the good and necessary changes are made automatically. True, Christ alone can transform the hearts of men and redeem them from sin and death. However, conversion is the beginning of a new life—a life filled with amazing potential. The Sermon on the Mount is a challenge to develop and discipline one's life. The Christian has the capacity for godly living and new heights of victory and joy unknown before Christ came into his heart. Jesus urges us to the habit of happiness.

One creates his world, the moods in which he wishes to live. If one is a sour old man or whining woman or a nagging wife or a bored youth—he is in the process of making himself what he wishes. Without Christ, life is gloomy; but with Him, life has great potential for happiness.

Billy Graham said, "All the Constitution guarantees is the pursuit of happiness. You have to catch up with it yourself." Yes, a man will decide for himself if he desires to be happy or not.

A minister of a mountain congregation told his people, "Smile. Christian's don't have to go around with long faces. I've seen Missouri mules with long faces that don't have a speck of religion."

In the light of the Beatitudes, a gloomy Christianity is unthinkable!

A man was visiting some friends. Though he was a sincere, dedicated Christian, his presence in the home made everyone uneasy. He made comments about the boy's length of hair, complained of the community's morals. Every subject he touched had the taint of criticism.

During the dinner, he was called away to the telephone. As soon as he shut the door, the daughter of the home whispered to the family, "Boy, is he bad news!"

Everyone understood and had a good chuckle. But one wonders how many Christians really are "bad news!" Many come across as unloving. Jesus' disciples are not called to police other people's standards and actions.

God said to Abraham, "And I will make of thee a great nation . . . and thou shalt be a blessing . . . and in thee shall all families of the earth be blessed" (Gen. 12:2-3). How about forming the habit of being a blessing to others?

A student once said of his Christian teacher, "She made me feel as if I were bathed in sunshine." Whoever the teacher was, she had caught the glory of Christ's loving ethic, the adventure of holy character.

A little girl was in a hospital ward at Christmastime. A pastor came to the ward and told the Christmas story to the children. The little girl had never heard it before. When the pastor left, she asked one of the nurses, "Did you ever hear that story about Jesus before?"

"Of course," she said. "I've heard it many times before."

"Well," said the girl, "you don't look as if you had."

The Christian is the person who has heard the Good News, and the Good News should make him happy.

The key word in the Beatitudes is the word "Blessed." The Greeks had a word for human happiness, but Jesus used this stronger word, *makarios*. It was a word the Greeks used only to describe the quality of joy reserved for the gods. Only the Christian can experience a godly happiness. That word, "blessed," in the Greek is made up of two smaller words that mean "not" and "fate" or "death." In other words, the Christian ought to be happy because he is immortal, not subject to the whims of fate. He is not under the influence of chance. He is guided by an all-wise Providence. God directs his steps to immortal glory.

This idea of "blessed" is not just a passing fancy, a temporary emotion of fun, but it expresses a permanent state and condition. The happiness we have in Christ is untouchable and is self-contained. It is a joy that is independent of all the chances and changes of life.

The child of God ought to live up to his potential happiness in Christ. Jesus remarked, "If ye know these things, happy *[makarioi]* are ye if ye do them" (John 13:17). Again, the Master said to His disciples, "Blessed *[makarioi]* are they that have not seen, and yet have believed" (John 20:29).

II

The Christian Discovers that Right Living Is Necessary for Happiness

One just can't live wrong and feel right! No one experiences this kind of happiness by accident. The disciple does not fall into this happiness nor lose it without cause. He cannot break the rules and expect to maintain happiness. Happiness for the Christian comes as the product of careful obedience.

The whole idea of the Beatitudes is a contradiction to the world's idea of happiness. Jesus underscored the character of the happy Christian, but our world can't understand it. The Beatitudes are a challenge to the world's accepted standards. This is a revolutionary recipe for happiness. Look at the contrasting popular notions of happiness:

> Blessed are the aggressive men: for they get on in the world.
> Blessed are the hard-boiled: for they never let life hurt them.
> Blessed are they who complain: for they get their own way in the end.
> Blessed are the blasé: for they never worry over their sins.
> Blessed are the slave drivers: for they get results.
> Blessed are the knowledgeable men of the world: for they know their way around.
> Blessed are the troublemakers: for they make people take notice of them.

However, Jesus described happiness as right living:

> Blessed are the poor in spirit: for theirs is the kingdom of heaven.
> Blessed are they that mourn: for they shall be comforted.
> Blessed are the meek: for they shall inherit the earth.
> Blessed are they which do hunger and thirst after righteousness: for they shall be filled.
> Blessed are the merciful: for they shall obtain mercy.
> Blessed are the pure in heart: for they shall see God.
> Blessed are the peacemakers: for they shall be called the children of God *(Matt. 5:3-9).*

Many people try the first set, but the result is a world full of unhappiness, greed, selfishness. The last set may not look very attractive and may seem unworkable, but those who have studied it and put it into practice find that life has abundant joy. What a way to live! These Beatitudes describe the man who has yielded himself in obedience to God's rule. This kind of blessedness or happiness comes from God and cannot be destroyed—even by persecution.

God honors obedience—the only kind of right living.

III

The Christian Experiences Happiness by the Law of Ebb and Flow

Did you notice the rhythm of the Beatitudes? For example, "Blessed are the merciful: for they shall obtain mercy." Here is the great law of the tides, of ebb and flow. The Scriptures talk about casting your bread on the waters, and it will come back. It is another way of describing action and reaction. As the tides go out, so will they come back. As one gives, so shall he receive. As one judges, so shall he be judged. He who would lose his life shall save it. This is a law that never fails.

Dr. Albert Schweitzer was asked, "Have you found happiness in Africa?"

He replied, "I have found service, and that is happiness enough for anyone."

Spiritual happiness—blessedness—is a climate of the soul. It is the perfume of righteous investment. It cannot be purchased or borrowed. Happiness is the by-product that comes from Christlike living. As one gives, he shall receive the unexpected joy!

IV

The Christian Builds His Happiness from the Inner Qualities of His Life—Not the Outward Circumstances

Jesus talks, not about conduct, but character! What one is inside, down deep, since being transformed by Christ's saving power, is what counts!

This blessedness is the result of an inner condition and not of an outer circumstance. Happiness is not a condition which one enters, but it is a fragrance that comes from the soul. Happiness is not the result of riding high on some emotional roller coaster. The blessing of God can be evident on the mountaintops of life and in the lonely canyons of dejection.

The disciple doesn't need to keep wishing for something to happen or for something to come his way to be happy. Happiness is a habit in this present life—right where you are. Someone wrote, "He who is not grateful for the good things he has would not be happy with what he wishes he had."

Since Christian joy comes from inner qualities of the soul, then outward circumstances cannot rob or destroy that happiness. Jesus said, "Your joy no man taketh from you" (John 16:22).

The follower of Christ need not merely react to outward circumstances. Externals do not have dominion over him. He can live in a climate of inner joy because Christ dwells within. The Beatitudes describe the kind of joy that sorrow, pain, and grief are powerless to invade. It is a joy which shines through tears, and which nothing in life or death can take away.

Many Christians are governed by their moods; they are thermometers, but others are thermostats! There is a basic difference between thermometers and thermostats. A thermometer merely tells what the temperature is. However, the thermostat controls the temperature. One can go through life just echoing the pressures and moods and climate around him—an unhappy calling. But he could cultivate the habit of happiness, setting the mood, determining actions and directions in life, creating a climate of Christian joy.

In the Ozark country of southern Missouri, two young boys were born and raised as neighbors. One lad lived on top of a rocky, knobby hill where the soil was rough and drained of fertility. The other lived on the rich, fertile bottomland. The first boy lived in poverty, while the second was reared in a wealthy family.

John grew up on the rocky hill where his father had been raised. With his father he had to scratch out a meager living. It was tough, hard work as they toiled over the impoverished land. The crops were scrubby—theirs was just a bare existence. Disappointment was a bitter cup from which they frequently drank.

In the lowland where Bill lived, the fields abounded. The corn was tall; the crops were lush and healthy.

The contrast disturbed John. When he would become melancholy and life seemed unbearable, he would find a certain rock where he could go and sit and look over Bill's fertile fields and gaze on the beauty below. John would think as he sat on his rock about how life had been cruel to him.

One day while he was sitting there, he saw Bill drive up in a brand-new yellow convertible. Deep inside he knew he would never have a yellow convertible if he worked all his life. He said to his father that night, "Dad, Bill has everything."

His father replied, "John, it depends on what you mean by 'everything.'"

In their senior year of high school, John's father died, so John was forced to quit school and work to support his mother and the younger children. Bill graduated and went on to the university to become a successful lawyer. The hometown folk heard rumors about Bill's success in the big city.

Meanwhile, John grubbed out a living on top of that knobby hill, fighting the rocks, trying to give his new wife, Rosemary, a better living than he had experienced. In time two boys were born to them.

Even then, when life seemed to close in on him, John would go to his "thinking rock." There, in his imagination, he built a beautiful house for Rosemary and the boys—but he knew they could never have such a house.

The years passed by. When John was in his mid-fifties, it seemed his trips out to the rock were more frequent. He would look at the bountiful fields below and be reminded he had never saved anything. His boys had been sent to college and that had drained him—but he had helped them through.

One day rumors circulated that Bill was coming back home. He was now a man in his mid-fifties also. His success had made possible an early retirement. Bill was coming back home to retire. When John heard the rumors, he went to the rock to think. He thought about Bill, the man who had everything—and now retiring at 55 years of age. John knew he could not retire at 65 or 75—probably never. It seemed life had been cruel to him.

With a heavy heart John went home. Rosemary met him at the door and said, "Honey, Bill has been here to see you. He wants to talk to you. He waited for an hour. I made him pancakes and gave him some buttermilk, but he finally left. You ought to go down and see him."

But John was not in the mood to go to see Bill. He just went back to his rock again and looked down at Bill's property, experiencing the misery he had known for a lifetime.

As he sat there, he heard a rustling behind him. There stood Bill. "Hello, John; it's been a long time, hasn't it?" said Bill.

John replied, "Yes, Bill, it has been a long time."

"John, I've thought about you for years and years, and I've wanted to come and have a talk with you. Do you know that I have envied you all through my life? Since I was a boy, I would go out into my backyard and look up at this rock. There you would sit. I envied you because I didn't have any kind of rock like that to sit on. Every friend I've ever had, John, I had because of something I possessed. You had your friends because of what you were.

"Your dad let you drive the tractor, but my dad would

never let me touch our tractor. Your dad let you go fishing with him, but my dad was too busy to go fishing. John, I find that nothing has changed now that we are 55.

"I saw Rosemary. I wish that I had a Rosemary, but I've been too busy to get married. My health has been broken, and that's the reason I've come back here—to see if I could get it back. John, you are a lucky man; you've always had everything. I hear one of your boys is a medical doctor and coming back to set up his practice in this community, and the other boy is in seminary planning to be a minister. You've always had everything and I've really had nothing.

"Say, John, let me tell you something else. Sometimes when I would look up here and see this rock with you sitting on it, there would be a little bit of mist or rain coming down that would cause a rainbow. It seems that this rock that you sat on was always at the end of the rainbow. John, you've not only had everything, but you have owned your own rainbow, too."

Yes, happiness is like a rainbow. When one chases it, he can never catch it. Many sit on rocks of self-pity and look down on others presumed to be more fortunate than themselves. And those people look back up and think, They sit at the foot of a rainbow.

Happiness is not a place; it is that beautiful climate of the Christ-filled, Christ-controlled life.

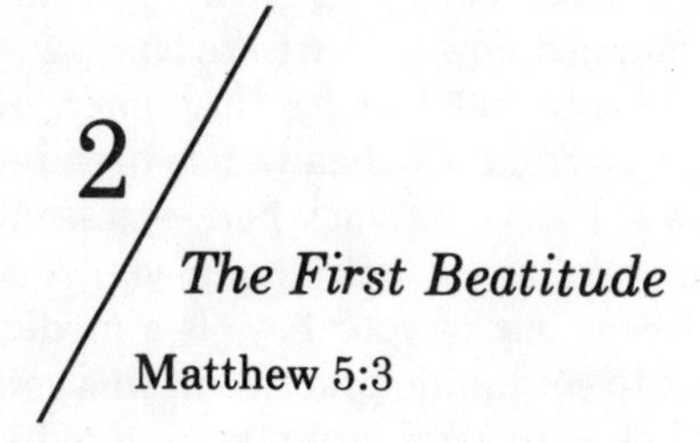

Pockets Inside Out

A man remarked one time, "It is a toss-up whether it is worse to be old and bent or young and broke."

Perhaps someday I will know for sure. Having been young and broke, I'm working toward the other end. It is easy for me to identify with poverty. Once, when I was a young boy, my mother decided to start giving me an allowance—5c a week. I kept records until she owed me $1.85; then I gave up on the whole program. Since getting married, my wife has been the treasurer, and she gives me an allowance. Now I get $5.00—but a haircut is $3.00!

My pockets have been periodically turned inside out —that last desperate search for the last cent. My trousers may be baggy and my shoes have holes in them—but I've got the cleanest pockets in town.

One night many years ago, my roommate in college, Jim Watt, and I stopped in Fresno at the Alaska Drive-in for a milkshake. As the carhop was approaching the car, I dug into my pockets—not a penny! I told Jim I was broke. He was used to that and grunted that he had enough to pay for it.

After drinking our milkshakes, Jim reached for his wallet. His pocket was empty. The wallet was at home on the dresser. Thus began a frantic search of the car. We cleaned out the glove compartment, the ashtrays, felt under the rugs, took out the seats—front and back. The thought occurred to us to leave the car and run away from embarrassment. However, we scraped up just enough pennies and nickels to pay the bill—but not a cent for a tip. Jim and I have laughed over that crazy incident for years. That was living on the sheer edge of poverty.

Jesus found a good ledge of rock, sat down with His disciples, and began His Sermon on the Mount by saying, "Blessed are the poor in spirit: for theirs is the kingdom of heaven" (Matt. 5:3). Since the first key to spiritual happiness is poverty, one is tempted to pass it off: "Well that one fits me. How about the next one?" But Jesus wasn't speaking of those who have had to turn their pockets inside out; He was speaking about "poverty of spirit."

The Master has called every Christian to be a pauper in the spirit. He does not ask of us what He was not willing to do. The Bible says, "Though he was rich, yet for your sakes he became poor, that ye through his poverty might be rich" (2 Cor. 8:9).

The poor in spirit are those who recognize their spiritual poverty. It describes those who are dependent upon God's grace, as compared to those who are worldly-minded, who take no thought of God during their busy lives.

When the Christian recognizes his own utter helplessness in earning God's favor, then he must put his complete trust in God's mercy through Christ. The hymn writer expressed it:

Just as I am, without one plea
But that Thy blood was shed for me.

That is the picture of a man standing before God with his pockets inside out. He has nothing to offer but himself. He has nothing to claim as a reason why God should let him into heaven—except that Jesus died for his sins. That is poverty of spirit.

In the Greek New Testament there are two words for "poor." One word describes the working man who has just enough to keep food on the table, clothes for the family, and a roof overhead—but nothing left over. He is just barely making ends meet. But the second word for "poor" suggests the fellow who has nothing—absolutely nothing. Completely destitute, he has no way to meet his basic needs. That is the word Jesus used here: "Blessed are the poor in spirit."

The Master was describing the spiritual condition in which a Christian has no earthly resources to save him, and who puts his whole trust in God. If one thinks that strange, just what does he have that can save his soul—except Christ? Jesus has not given a command—just an exclamation of the joy one has who trusts completely in Christ: "O the blessedness of the poor in spirit!"[1] This is not an option for the Christian. It is the only way into the kingdom of heaven.

I

The Poor in Spirit Are Conscious of Spiritual Dependence

Jesus said, "How blest are those who know that they are poor" (Matt. 5:3, NEB). Kenneth Wuest translates it: "Spiritually prosperous are the destitute and helpless in the realm of the Spirit."[2] Goodspeed gives us a clear view of its meaning: "Blessed are those who feel their spiritual need."

Jesus' phrase "poor in spirit" is not to be confused

with the idea of those who have a poor spirit—a negative, miserable, unhappy attitude. The Master praises those who feel their spiritual poverty—who recognize their dependence upon God. When one becomes a Christian, he is very much aware that he needs Christ—desperately. But that dependency does not change. When one is poor in spirit, he admits Christ's continued presence is what he needs.

A missionary to the New Hebrides Islands was working diligently on translating the Bible into the native language. While he was searching for the appropriate word for "trusting" or "believing," it seemed to evade his understanding.

One day he called in the home of a native Christian and sat down on a chair. He said to the woman, "What am I doing?"

She replied in her language, "You are resting."

The missionary recognized that word, but it wasn't what he was searching for. He lifted both feet off the ground and put them on the rungs of the chair. Again he asked, "What am I doing now?"

The woman remarked again in her language, "O sir, you are resting wholly, you are trusting." The new word to the missionary's ears meant "to set one's whole weight upon." That was the word he needed to describe trusting in Christ—with both feet off the ground: setting his whole weight upon Jesus!

The man who puts his whole weight on Jesus will find two things happening to himself. First, he will become detached from things. He will not find his happiness in material possessions. "Things" are so temporal, so fleeting. One Sunday morning I got word that my uncle's beautiful, commodious home had burned to the ground. I couldn't help but think what a tragedy it is if one invests his whole life in material possessions. How imperative it is to invest "where neither moth nor rust doth corrupt, and where thieves do not break through nor steal" (Matt. 6:20).

Secondly, the man who puts his whole weight on Jesus becomes attached to God. God can bring help and direction to life. A cellar wall in Cologne bears the following inscription, etched there by someone during the Nazi terror: "I believe in the sun, even when it is not shining. I believe in love, even when feeling it not. I believe in God, even when He is silent."

When nothing whereon to lean remains,
When strongholds crumble to dust;
When nothing is sure but that God still reigns,
That is just the time to trust.

—Ruth B. Teasdale

What a joy to depend on God instead of ourselves!

II

The Poor in Spirit Have Been Cleansed of Pride

J. B. Phillips translates the first beatitude: "How happy are those who know their need for God, for the kingdom of Heaven is theirs" (Matt. 5:3).

Pride is an expensive vice. One man's wife cried, "O John, that lady next door has a hat just like mine!"

"Well," sighed the husband, "I suppose that means you want to buy another hat."

She replied, "Well, it would be cheaper than moving."

Poverty of spirit is the result of dethroning selfish pride. When Christ comes into a man's life, pride is immediately under attack. Pride is the sin of dethroning God from His rightful sovereignty in a man's soul. For a man to be proud, he really has to be kidding himself. If one is honest with himself and with God, he will be poor in spirit. Cervantes wrote, "A knowledge of yourself will preserve you from vanity." It is certainly true in the spiritual realm.

Pride limits spiritual growth. The one who is poor in spirit—humble—is in a position to expand his soul. He knows and admits his spiritual poverty.

Mrs. Perkins attended a small country church. After each sermon, she would greet the pastor with these words: "That certainly was a good message, Pastor. They sure did need it."

Her spiritual pride would not allow the message to help her grow and mature. However, one snowy morning no one but Mrs. Perkins came to church. The pastor thought he had a good chance this time: "Mrs. Perkins, sit down. I'm going to deliver my sermon anyway—to you!"

He preached on the sin of pride for half an hour. When he finished, she commented: "My, that was a fine message, Pastor. If they'd been here, they sure would have got it!"

Jesus stands at the opposite end. He speaks of the way of self-renunciation, self-abandonment. He calls, "If any man will come after me, let him deny himself [literally, 'utterly reject himself,' comments E. Stanley Jones], and take up his cross, and follow me." Self-pride must be renounced.

Dr. Jones tells of watching a poor, unhappy bird beating himself for hours against a mirror. The angry bird was fighting his own reflection. Suddenly he stopped. Listened. He seemed to hear the call of the great outdoors. He quit fighting himself and flew away. Dr. Jones later saw the bird out in the garden and heard him singing, joyously at peace with himself and in harmony with the world.[3]

The call of Christ comes to men who are fighting themselves—angry and unhappy men. He says, "Happy is the man who is renounced in spirit." He beckons him into the garden of a restored paradise—at peace with himself and in tune with God and His kingdom.

The *Amplified Bible* describes the "poor in spirit" as:

"the humble, rating themselves insignificant." Someone said, "When I have my eyes on God, I feel small but adequate; when I have my eyes on myself, I feel large but insecure."

For the Christian, the attitude of the poor in spirit is not a self-deprecating attitude. It is not a sense of worthlessness, for real humility recognizes one's true worth in Christ. Peter says, "You are the chosen race, the King's priests, the holy nation, God's own people, chosen to proclaim the wonderful acts of God, who called you from the darkness into his own marvelous light" (1 Peter 2:9, TEV).

In the midst of a difficult rehearsal of Beethoven's Ninth Symphony, Toscanini said to the orchestra: "Who am I? Who is Toscanini? I am nobody! Who are you? You are nobody. I am nobody and you are nobody." He stood taut and silent. Then the conductor whispered, "It is Beethoven. He is everything!"

To the poor in spirit, "Christ is everything!"

III

The Poor in Spirit Have a Right to Claim the Kingdom of Heaven Now

In the *Living Bible,* Jesus is quoted as saying, "Humble men are very fortunate! . . . for the Kingdom of Heaven is given to them!" (Matt. 5:3, TLB).

No translation has "for theirs *shall be* the kingdom of heaven." The Kingdom is a present reality. After all, there is no one in the kingdom of God who is not poor in spirit. The attitude of total dependence upon God is necessary for entrance into the kingdom of heaven. Those who are the poor in spirit are at present in God's kingdom.

A literary study of the Beatitudes reveals that they are in the form of what is called "synthetic parallelism." It is a type of Hebrew poetry in which the second line of the poem completes the first line by another definition. The second line describes the first. "O the blessedness of the poor in spirit"—that line is defined by the phrase "for theirs is the kingdom of heaven." The reason the poor in spirit are joyous is because they are in God's kingdom!

These are not some religious-sounding hopes for the future. They are up-to-date congratulations on what is reality now! Christ's kingdom is an immediate possession. It is not a distant place, but an experience in this life. The kingdom of heaven is not something we are going to enter some day; we have already entered.

Jesus gave a good definition of His kingdom in the Lord's Prayer: "Thy kingdom come. Thy will be done in earth, as it is in heaven" (Matt. 6:10). Here again is the same poetic form as in the Beatitudes. Therefore the kingdom of God is where God's will is done. The kingdom of heaven is the reign of God in the Christian's heart and life.

We who are so destitute, with our spiritual pockets inside out, have reason to rejoice—we have gained a Kingdom with Christ.

Fritz Kreisler was one of the world's most famous violinists. One time he visited a man who owned a rare violin. The owner had been so overprotective he never let anyone touch it. However, he finally consented to let Kreisler play it.

As the master violinist began to perform, it was as though the violin came to life and sang like an angel. The musical notes floated like the fragrance of orange blossoms on a warm spring night. The owner stood listening, enraptured in sonic delight. He never dreamed his violin had such depth of tone. When Kreisler finished his performance, the owner said to the artist: "Take it. It belongs to you. You can do more with it than I can."

These are the words the poor in spirit utters to the Master: "Here is my life. Take it. It belongs to You. You can do more with it than I can."

3

The Second Beatitude

Matthew 5:4

No Anesthetic, Please

A young medical doctor began his practice in a small town. His first patient was an old man who gave in great detail all the symptoms of his ailments. The doctor was doing his best to diagnose the old man's problem, but he didn't have the foggiest idea what was wrong. With his best medical voice, he asked, "Have you ever had this trouble before?"

The old man replied, "Sure, many times!"

Drawing upon his thorough training, the young physician said, "Well, you have it again!"

Whatever it is that creates confusion, frustration, guilt, sadness, our old world sure has it again! Christians must not be unfeeling about the sin and heartache of our world. They must care—and care deeply. Jesus makes this strange statement: "Blessed are they that mourn: for they shall be comforted" (Matt. 5:4). This kind of mourning comes from a heart that is sensitive to spiritual things. Only the Christian who feels deeply can mourn.

Charles L. Allen tells the story of Father Damien, who

was a missionary for 13 years in a leper colony. One day he spilled boiling water on his foot—but there was no pain at all. He knew suddenly he had contracted the terrible disease of leprosy. It would have been better if the boiling water had caused him great pain.[1] There is a spiritual state in which many people are past feeling. Spiritual insensitivity is a sign of the dread dominion of sin.

"Blessed are they that mourn." Our world finds this statement absurd. Think of it: "Happy are those who mourn!" The world does its best to shun grief. If one takes the pulse of society, the advice is given: "Forget your troubles, turn your back upon them, do everything you can not to face them. . . . Be as happy as you can."[2]

In many ways people try to desensitize themselves from reality. In spite of many attempted escape routes, Jesus calls for us to face life—the good and the bad—without spiritual anesthetics. On the cruel Cross outside Jerusalem, Jesus refused to take the medication that would dull the pain and agony. He was spiritually sensitive to the great moment of atonement.

In this second beatitude, Jesus calls every Christian to become spiritually sensitive. The Master's men in our day must not be dulled by pleasure nor lulled by materialism. Our generation needs Christian men, Spirit-filled men, who are alert with great feeling to the pulse of our world. This is no time to be glassy-eyed daydreamers. "Blessed are they that mourn: for they shall be comforted."

Jesus tells us two great things here.

I

Happiness Comes to Those Who Are Spiritually Sensitive

This word "mourn" is an intense word. Not the momentary twinge of sadness that passes with a nod, it is the mourning of a broken heart, such as accompanies the bereavement of a loved one. It brings uncontrolled tears to the eyes. The Christian is a man capable of tremendous sensitivity.

The spiritually sensitive person takes sin seriously. Blessed is the man who is deeply repentant for his sins. He realizes in part the high price God paid through Jesus Christ for his sin. He is heartbroken over the stain of sin and the scars of the soul. Sin is no trivial affair. While other people may be content with an unexamined life, the mourner, seeing God's grieving love, cries out, "God be merciful to me a sinner" (Luke 18:13). Being spiritually sensitive, the Christian knows that the reverse side of his remorse for sin is the sweet presence of God.

A father told his son that conscience is a small voice that talks to us when we have done wrong. The small boy prayed, "O God, make the little voice loud!"

The Christian mourns for God's voice to speak clearly and repeatedly. For while he is tempted to sin, down deep in his soul he doesn't want to strike out against God's will. Not far along in the Christian walk one begins to discover that he himself is the problem—and Jesus came to save him from himself! He wants to deal with the selfishness, prejudice, status-seeking, power struggles, hostility, and violence.

If one doesn't take the problem of sin seriously, he will become spiritually numb. Recognizing his need for God's power to overcome sin, one must be honest to admit he cannot correct the problem by himself.

Myron Augsburger tells the following story about a man who was shopping in a supermarket.

> [He was] pushing a cart down the aisle between the stacks of groceries with a little boy in the basket of the cart crying insistently. A lady heard the man talking as he went along, "Keep calm, Albert, don't make a scene,

> Albert." Some minutes later she was at the check-out counter when he came up, cart piled high with groceries, child still crying, and the man speaking emphatically in low tones, "Keep calm, Albert; don't make a scene. Control yourself, Albert." The lady said, "Sir, I'm amazed at how calmly you keep speaking to that child when he doesn't pay any attention to you." The man replied, "Lady, you don't understand—I'm Albert!"[3]

Taking the sin problem seriously, one should bring it to God for deliverance. Calvary is the proof that sin troubled God. Has it troubled you?

The spiritually sensitive person is compassionate toward others. Blessed is the man who voluntarily shares his neighbor's suffering. Though he could easily avoid it, the Christian can never say, "It is not my business. I have enough troubles of my own." He refuses that kind of spiritual anesthetic that pretends sorrow does not exist. The Christian mourns because he exposes himself to the world's misery—with compassion.

Had Peter and John not been sensitive to the spiritual needs of others, they might have said to the beggar at the gate called Beautiful, "Silver and gold have I none, but I'd be delighted to direct you to the welfare office." The disciple of Jesus weeps with those who weep. He looks at perishing souls with compassion as Jesus did over Jerusalem!

A little girl came home from a neighbor's house where her little friend had died.

"Why did you go?" asked her father.

"To comfort her mother," replied the child.

"What could you do to comfort her?"

"I climbed into her lap and cried with her!" was the reply.

The Christian may not have all the right words—but he has the deep feelings. Christianity is caring! Blessed is the man who cares intensely for the sufferings, sorrows, and needs of others. Dr. Bob Pierce has been quoted as praying, "Let my heart be broken with the things that break the heart of God."

This kind of religion is no escape mechanism. It is not a way out of pain and sorrow. Here is a religion of involvment—not escape. "How blest are the sorrowful; they shall find consolation" (Matt. 5:4, NEB). While it may seem odd to others, the happiest people in the world are those who choose to care until it hurts. The most miserable people in the world are those who center upon themselves, who deliberately shun the cares of others. Happiness eludes them. They save their lives but they lose life. The Spirit-filled Christian is never at home detached from people.

William Barclay summarizes the second beatitude: "O the bliss of the man whose heart is broken for the world's suffering and for his own sin, for out of his sorrow he will find the joy of God!"[4]

II

Comfort Comes to Those Who Are Spiritually Sensitive

"Blessed are they that mourn: for they shall be comforted." The Christian, sensitive to his own deep needs, is intensely compassionate towards others and soon discovers he must have strength beyond himself. A newspaper noted, "When we're weak, we usually need outside help—it doesn't help much to give one arm a transfusion from the other." God has provided a comfort, a strengthening for His people.

David Livingstone, pioneer missionary to the continent of Africa, once said when passing through a difficult situation: "I felt the down-reach of the Divine." When we sincerely try and trust, we too feel that glorious new strength—"the down-reach of the Divine."

The Bible says, "Be afflicted, and mourn, and weep: let your laughter be turned to mourning, and your joy to heaviness. Humble yourselves in the sight of the Lord, and he shall lift you up" (Jas. 4:9-10).

Comfort comes because the spiritually sensitive person is called alongside of Christ. The phrase "They shall be comforted" is one long word in the Greek that comes from two simple words: "near" and "I call." In other words, Jesus calls them to himself, to be with Him, to remain near Him. He is the great Encourager who speaks words of pardon, peace, and zest into the soul. His great invitation to the common man has always been "Come unto me, all ye that labour and are heavy laden, and I will give you rest" (Matt. 11:28). The spiritually sensitive Christian is called to the side of Jesus. But this comfort is no soothing, soft thing. While it is tenderness, it is also reinforcement in the face of rugged living.

"Happy are those who know what sorrow means, for they will be given courage and comfort" (Matt. 5:4, Phillips). The English word *comfort* is made up of two words: *con* ("with") and *fortis* ("strength"). Literally it means "strengthened by being with." One will be strengthened by being with Jesus. He takes all of our infirmities, failures, frustrations, and, when we yield them to Him, He brings encouragement and fixes us up for victorious, godly living.

Benjamin West became one of Britain's great artists. While he was a young boy baby-sitting his little sister, Sally, he decided to paint a picture of her. With his colored ink he set to work—but chaos came from his brush. Ink was everywhere. The picture was a disaster.

When his mother came home, she quickly understood what he had been trying to do. With a tone of delight, the mother said, "Look at that! A picture of Sally!" She lifted little Benjamin in her arms and gave him a kiss of triumph.

Benjamin West said throughout his artistic career: "My mother's kiss made me a painter!"

Jesus sees our imperfections, our inadequacies, but He also sees our motives, our deep desires to please Him. He not only accepts us as we are, but He gives us the encouragement to become something better, to be fruitful, to become an artisan of God's great grace!

Paul rejoiced, "Blessed be God, even the Father of our Lord Jesus Christ, the Father of mercies, and the God of all comfort; who comforteth us in all our tribulation, that we may be able to comfort them which are in any trouble, by the comfort wherewith we ourselves are comforted of God. For as the sufferings of Christ abound in us, so our consolation also aboundeth by Christ" (2 Cor. 1:3-5).

Peter Marshall gave this thrilling illustration in one of his unique sermons:

> There is a lovely story about George Washington when he took command of the Continental Army at Cambridge, Mass. He found a ragged body of soldiers. Some of them had uniforms, some had none.
>
> Some had guns.
> Some had sticks.
> Others had only the implements which they had brought from their farms.
>
> A regiment from Connecticut looked particularly untidy. The men were few
> badly armed
> and poorly dressed.
>
> They did not even stand at attention. Their ranks were ragged, and they had the air of discouragement. Many of them were hungry and had gone without a decent meal for days on end.
>
> Some were lame. They were a sorry lot.
>
> Yet when the regiment was drawn up for Washington to inspect them, the great general stood erect and, looking at them as if they were in the finest regiment in the world, he said:

> "Gentlemen, I have great confidence in the men of Connecticut."

One of the soldiers writing home to his family, said in his letter,

> "When I heard Washington say that, I clasped my musket to my breast and said to myself,
> 'Let them come on.'"[5]

In the face of spiritual opposition, "Let us therefore come boldly unto the throne of grace, that we may obtain mercy, and find grace to help in time of need" (Heb. 4:16).

Comfort comes because the spiritually sensitive person is aware of a great future. When Jesus was asked to give the sermon in His home synagogue, He selected a passage from Isaiah as the text. In it He read these words: "The Spirit of the Lord God is upon me; because the Lord hath anointed me to preach good tidings unto the meek; . . . to comfort all that mourn" (Isa. 61:1-2). That day Jesus said this scripture had begun to be fulfilled, and it leads to the great day of the "consolation of Israel," the future coming day of the Lord. The Christian should receive comfort and encouragement in the fact that there is coming a marvelous day when we shall see Jesus face-to-face. We shall be gathered into mansions of glory prepared for those that love Him and wait for His blessed appearing.

When Jesus said, "They shall be comforted," it was a promise partially fulfilled in the mighty acts of redemption at the Cross and the victorious resurrection of Jesus, followed by the gift of the Holy Spirit. But it is a promise to be completely fulfilled when sin and death shall be done away and "God will wipe away every tear from their eyes" (Rev. 7:17, TEV).

For those who know what spiritual mourning is, heaven becomes greatly anticipated. One psalm has given many Christian workers encouragement through the years: "They that sow in tears shall reap in joy. He that goeth forth and weepeth, bearing precious seed, shall doubtless come again with rejoicing, bringing his sheaves with him" (Ps. 126:5-6). Heaven will be a harvest of joy. What returns on the seedtime of tears in this life! Paul said, "For I reckon that the sufferings of this present time are not worthy to be compared with the glory which shall be revealed in us" (Rom. 8:18).

What a future! Whether this life becomes all one desires or not, God has a great tomorrow. This present moment of testing opens into a millennium of everlasting joy. "Spiritually prosperous are those who are mourning, because they themselves shall be encouraged and strengthened by consolation" (Matt. 5:4, Wuest).

There may be moments of discouragement, but they usually come when one loses sight of the eternal verities and God's promise for a great future.

Abraham Lincoln was staying in the home of a farmer in Illinois. During the night, an unusual number of shooting stars were seen streaking across the black velvet sky. The farmer was frightened and awakened Lincoln. "Abe, get up! Look out the window! The world is coming to an end!"

Lincoln stretched out his long, lanky body and went to the window. He stuck his head out and looked at the celestial demonstration. He grinned and put his arm around the frightened farmer. "Don't be alarmed. Go back to bed. There may be some shooting stars, but the great constellations still stand."

If upheavals and conflicts arise in one's life, he can give thanks to Almighty God that His great constellations still stand. The outlook for the future with Him is not an unhappy one. He reminds each one, "Heaven and earth may pass away, but my words shall not pass away" (Matt. 24:35). There is comfort in God's unchanging certainties!

4

The Third Beatitude

Matthew 5:5

God's Gentleman

The man admitted, "I used to be proud. But no more. Now I'm perfect!"

To be conscious of one's humility is to be unconscious of one's pride.

At a somewhat early age, people learn that survival seems to depend on aggression. With the thin skin of arrogance, men camouflage their insecurities—pretending to be something they aren't. Wracked by the fear of discovery, most cannot admit to themselves what emptiness lurks below the surface of the conscious mind. If there could be but one word to describe the natural man, the word is *pretense.* So many mental, spiritual, and physical disorders can be traced directly to this problem.

Most people are like the little boy whose mother referred to him as her "little lamb."

When he got enough courage to say so, he said,

"Mother, I don't want to be your little lamb. I want to be your little tiger."[1]

Many Christians think that aggression is the way to succeed and survive in this kind of world. But Jesus shocks us with the words "Blessed are the meek: for they shall inherit the earth" (Matt. 5:5). The Master Teacher was simply quoting from the Psalms: "But the meek shall inherit the earth; and shall delight themselves in the abundance of peace" (37:11). Like so many other times, Jesus brought Old Testament truths into focus. He did more than say it —He demonstrated it. If one desires to see what meekness means, he can look at Jesus. He lived it on every page of the four Gospels.

The strange quirks of living languages change meanings and usages of words. The word *meek* has been made bankrupt for the English reader. The closest thing to our present word *meekness* is probably *mousy*. There is nothing spiritual about fearfulness, timidity, and living in a hole!

The French versions of the Bible use a word we all know: "Blessed are the *débonnaire.*" This carries the idea of gladness—not the false sadness popularly linked to *meek.* The debonair man is overcome by God's greatness and goodness. He counts his own life as nothing, simply because he is happily living for love's sake. The Greek word translated *"débonnaire"* means "goodwill toward men and reverent obedience toward God."[2]

The meek man is not someone who has scratched everything good and bad out of his life and, with a note of sadness, has "nothing left but God." Many have gone that dead-end street to spirituality—only to find just another alley of pride with all of its litter. The meek man is so full of zest and joy in serving God, loving men for Christ's sake, that he overlooks himself in the process.

"Blessed are the meek"! There is a word in English that once really expressed what Jesus was saying: *Gentleman.* "Blessed is the gentleman: for he shall inherit the earth." That's a good antidote to the crass crudeness that sometimes passes as spirituality in the raw. The disciple of Jesus is to be a gentleman in every arena of life.

I

God's Gentleman Has Strength Under Control

Meekness is not the absence of strength, but the restraint of strength.

Matthew put the Beatitudes at the front of his Gospel story of Jesus for a reason. He wrote his Gospel for the Jews. They had the idea that the kingdom of God was a materialistic and militaristic conquest. To them the Messiah would be a great general and king who would lead them to a physical, violent victory over the world. Immediately, Jesus dismisses that kind of kingdom. The quality of life in His kingdom was not unbridled strength, but that of a gentleman who has his life under control. God's gentleman is not harsh, self-assertive, aggressive, covetous, or trampling over others in brute force. He is not a shock trooper for God, but an ambassador.

A look at Jesus shows He was strong and manly. When the Master was arrested and dragged through the insults of His trial and crucifixion, He did not demonstrate weakness at all: "When he was reviled, reviled not again; when he suffered, he threatened not; but committed himself to him that judgeth righteously" (1 Pet. 2:23).

The Greeks defined virtues as the middle between two extremes. Aristotle defined meekness as the middle between excessive anger and excessive angerlessness. "It is the happy medium between too much and too little anger."[3] This kind of meekness is the power to be angry along with the power to restrain that anger. It is the power to desire something along with the power to relinquish it if it is best.

Jesus never was angered by what someone did to Him, but He did demonstrate anger against what someone did to others. There is a selfish anger that is a sin, but there is a selfless anger that is one of the great moral dynamics of our world. Without it, there would be moral collapse. Among Christians, this selfless anger should find expression in defending the right and good.

Admittedly there are people who appear to be meek but are not. If one gets to know them well, one finds they are anything but meek. They are just lazy. The Bible never advocates lethargy. Meekness is not flabbiness. Some people are just easygoing. That is not meekness. It is emotional flabbiness. It is a spirit of compromise or peace at any price. Many folk think that anything is better than disagreement—just smooth over the little things that divide, and let's all be nice and happy. But that is moral cowardice—not meekness. One can be sure that if a group of people agree all the time on everything, some of them either are not thinking or are inwardly about to explode!

Meekness is not just being nice. Some people are just born nice—but that has nothing to do with the spiritual quality of meekness. One dog is nicer than another; one cat is nicer than another. It is biological and environmental. But Jesus is talking about a wonderful quality of the new birth!

This meekness is compatible with strength—great strength. It is compatible with great authority and power. The martyrs of the Christian faith were meek but never weak! They had a courage, poise, and an inner strength that circumstances could not take away.

II

God's Gentleman Has a Spiritual Endowment

This meekness is not merely a natural temperament. It has to do with an inward spirit of the born-again disciple of Jesus.

All Christians are meant to have this quality of Kingdom living. So it is not a natural disposition, because we all are quite different. Every Christian, regardless of his natural temperament, is meant to be meek, a quality produced only by the Spirit of God.

Like anything genuine, there are counterfeits. Like all counterfeits, someday people will know the difference between the phony and the real. Someone said, "Sincere humility attracts. Lack of humility subtracts. Artificial humility detracts."

History is laden with poor folk who went off alone to make themselves meek—but for nothing! Only the Holy Spirit can make one truly meek; no one but the Holy Spirit can make us poor in spirit. Paul tells us, "Let this mind be in you, which was also in Christ Jesus" (Phil. 2:5). Philippians 2:6-8 describes how Jesus gave up His glory in heaven; He did not cling to His right of equality with God. He deliberately gave it all up to come and walk among men. God's will for us is our testing ground for meekness. We need to rehearse in the little things of life: "Yes, Lord. Yes, Lord." When the gigantic decisions come, we will be ready to whisper beneath the load, "Yes, Lord. Yes, Lord."

One must learn to trust God for this quality of life. He has promised to give it. "Blessed are the meek," not those who trust in their own strength, powers, and abilities. God's gentleman has been endowed with a spirit that is willing to be God-controlled, rather than self-controlled. God's gentleman is not weak or cowardly. He has learned under the pressures of life to stand before the grace and greatness of God. As a new man, a new creation, he belongs to an entirely different Kingdom. Not only is the world unlike him, but it cannot possibly understand him.

The Greek word *praus,* translated "meekness," is also used to describe an animal that has become domesticated. *Praus* suggests the animal that can respond to a word of command or answer to the reins of the bridle. It is the word for one who has learned to accept control.[4] One can never accept nor understand himself until he responds to God's whisper or control and accepts His authority and lordship over his life.

The Hebrew word which is readily translated "meek" really means "to be molded." Molded by whom? God!

Have Thine own way, Lord! Have Thine own way!
Thou art the Potter; I am the clay.
Mold me and make me after Thy will,
While I am waiting, yielded and still.

III

God's Gentleman Has Been Set Free Indeed!

"Blessed are the meek: for they shall inherit the earth"! There's no need to scramble over the necks of others, no need to prove a point—God's world is our inheritance! The reward of eternal life is a legacy, a gift. We cannot earn it. We do not have to wrest the center stage away from others, for we are the children of God. The best in life is ours for the asking! That word "inherit" implies membership in God's family. We are the children of the King! In the things that count, we have an eternal inheritance!

Norman Vincent Peale said in a sermon, "The Christian religion is far greater than anyone realizes. It tells weak people they can become strong. It tells defeated people they can be victorious. It tells unhappy, mixed-up people they can become organized. It teaches that we can be great persons. It teaches that we can live tremendous lives. It teaches that we can build a wonderful world. There is nothing like it in the whole wide world.

"Listen to just this one statement from Jeremiah: 'Call unto me, and I will answer thee, and shew thee great and mighty things, which thou knowest not' (Jer. 33:3). Call upon God, it says, and He will answer; He will show you tremendous things. And yet we make something small and indifferent out of our religion."

Since God's gentleman has strength on reserve and has an inheritance of God, he no longer has to suffer at the image of self. Most people are in quiet anguish over their inferiorities, their limitations, their shortcomings. That is a trick of the devil. If one were asked to write a list of his good, strong points, most people would sit and scratch around—maybe jot down one or two things. But if asked to write down his limitations, weak points, etc., he could readily fill a page. Jesus came to set us free from that stupid, lopsided, thwarted view of ourselves. It seems most people are locked in a box of their own construction—that's hardly inheriting the earth! God has done a wonderful work in redemption. He has a plan to set us free from our own destruction. When one realizes he is a child of God, that ought to get him out of a pauper's state of mind.

The English word for *meek* comes from the old Anglo-Saxon *mecca*. It meant "companion" or "equal." God's gentleman is able to readily associate with anyone, feeling neither superior nor inferior to anyone. The man who is meek is not overly sensitive about himself. He isn't always watching himself to be sure he's OK! He isn't always on the defensive. No longer does he worry about himself or what other people are saying about him. Self-pity finds no foothold, because he is not sorry for himself. He knows who he is and where he is going!

Bertha Munro wrote, "Humility is not thinking yourself little, but thinking little of yourself." Many Christians are rather good at thinking themselves little and insignificant, but what an insult to God's redeeming grace! He has made them new creatures in Christ Jesus—and He does all things well. Disciples should quit dragging their redeemed lives through the mud of inferiority! Paul said, "I can do everything through him who gives me strength" (Phil. 4:13, NIV). That's God's gentleman! That's the real meaning of meekness!

Too many people have such a terrible view of themselves that they are afraid to risk failure. Most people have heard of Babe Ruth, the one-time home-run king of baseball. But Babe Ruth was also strikeout king! He tried harder than anyone else and failed more than anyone else —but he won lasting fame in his profession.

One of the favorite sports stories happened during a World Series baseball game many years ago. It was the fifth inning and the score was tied 4-4 between the New York Yankees and the Chicago Cubs. Babe Ruth stepped up to bat. The Cub pitcher threw the ball right across the heart of the plate. Ruth watched it go by. The crowd laughed and booed. He put up one finger for strike one! That irked the pitcher, and he got careless and threw a ball. Again Ruth signaled with his fingers—one and one. With incredible speed the ball sizzled over the plate. A second strike. Then another ball. The count was 2-2. The crowd was tense. Was Babe Ruth about to strike out? He was relaxed. He walked around home plate. He picked up some dust, spat on his hands, and rubbed them on his pant legs. He pounded the bat on the ground and walked up to the plate.

Suddenly he pointed his finger to the center-field

fence, indicating where he intended to send the ball. The infuriated Cub pitcher sent the ball right over the plate. There was the crack of the bat. The ball flew over the center-field fence—a prodigious home run. Babe Ruth jogged around the bases amid the applause and cheers of his teammates and the crowd.

Later a newspaperman asked him, "But what if you hadn't hit that ball, after signaling where it was going to go?"

A look of astonishment crossed his face. "Not hit it? Why, I never even thought of such a thing!"

God's gentleman is not limited by negative, failure complexes. He knows that "all things work together for good to them that love God" (Rom. 8:28). There's no point in cringing from fear of failure! So what if there is a failure along the way? That's one good way to learn. Meekness always implies a teachable spirit. "Blessed are the meek: for they shall inherit the earth"! God's gentleman is blessed because he has the most comfortable, undisturbed enjoyment of self, of friends, of God. He is fit to live and fit to die!

Paganini was a genius on the violin. One night the maestro was playing before a huge audience in Italy. During the concert, a string on his violin snapped. Broken! Momentarily the crowd was startled, but he continued to play on the remaining three strings. Then another string broke—but still he played. The impossible happened! A third string broke! The audience was aghast! Did Paganini give up? Did he write off the performance as a flop?

Paganini was confident. He knew his instrument and that he was master of it. He would give it his best. Raising his Stradivarius violin up high, he shouted, "One string—and Paganini!" Paganini proceeded to play the concert on that one string with such skill that the audience gave him a thunderous, standing ovation.

There are times in life when one string breaks, and another, and another, until it will seem everything is against us. But if one is a child of God, he has an inheritance from the King. He can stand tall and remind himself, "In quietness and in confidence shall be your strength" (Isa. 30:15).

Kenneth Taylor paraphrases this portion with enthusiasm: "The meek and lowly are fortunate! for the whole wide world belongs to them" (Matt. 5:5, TLB).

5

The Fourth Beatitude

Matthew 5:6

The Whole Thing

A halfhearted Christian attempts to serve Christ without offending the devil. But the real disciple can never be thoroughly satisfied with partial goodness. If one is going to walk with Jesus in the light of God's Word, he will go the whole way. A recent popular television advertisement showed a man despairingly surprised he had eaten the "whole thing"! But in the Christian life it is no surprise. Holy, saintly lives are not an accident of temperament or good upbringing. As has been said, "Man has been created with a God-shaped vacuum in his soul, and nothing but God can fill it." He has wonderfully given every Christian the desire for righteousness—the whole thing.

In the first three beatitudes, Jesus spoke about the stage of recognizing spiritual poverty and dependence, of an emptying process of self, but now He comes to the positive side. The Lord speaks plainly that those who are emptied and ready for God's use can be filled with God's righteousness.

I

The Christian Becomes Aware of His Need for God's Righteousness

Good actions and good intentions do not meet the majestic demands of Kingdom living. Somehow there is an empty ring when one strives in his own strength to succeed for God.

Incomplete without God, man was never intended to be strong in his own might. Created in the image of God, man was designed to have fellowship with God, and his life is incomplete apart from God. One cannot fulfill his potential as a child of God without allowing the Lord to work in his life.

Dr. Adler was a self-sufficient, proud man, an educated professor. One time he attended a dinner party, and the conversation turned into a debate. Everyone disagreed with him, so he got up and stormed out the door in a rage. He vented his anger by slamming the door behind him.

There was an embarrassing silence in the room for a few moments. One woman sighed with relief, "Well, he's gone!"

The hostess replied, "No, he isn't; that's a closet!"

Slamming independently out of God's presence only closes one into a narrower existence.[1]

Not only are we incomplete without God, but our righteousness is inadequate. As long as we think in terms of what we ourselves can do, there will be nothing but failure, frustration, and fear. When we begin to think, Not I, but Christ in me, then comes peace and spiritual power.

Suddenly we are aware that we need the righteousness of Christ. It was our own sins that separated us from God, and only through His forgiving grace in Christ can that be remedied. Jesus is our Righteousness. He alone can put us in a right relationship with God. There aren't enough laws to keep a man righteous in God's sight. We must live in the righteousness that Christ has provided for us. When we are justified by faith, we are put into a right relationship with God. In this right relationship we live a life that expresses the life of Christ in us. Ian Thomas said, "Godliness—or God-likeness—is the direct and exclusive consequence of God's activity in man. Not the consequence of your capacity to imitate God, but the consequence of God's capacity to reproduce Himself in you!"[2]

A famous violinist performed before a huge concert audience. At the close of the first movement, to the amazement of the audience, he smashed the violin on the floor. In the startled silence, he stepped forward and said, "Don't be upset. That violin is just a cheap one I got for a few dollars. Now listen to the Stradivarius violin." Quickly tuning his expensive violin, he continued the concert. However majestic the music, most people couldn't tell the difference. At the conclusion, he said to the audience: "Many critics have said that the beauty of the music was due to the expensive violin. I have demonstrated for you that the music is not in the instrument but in the one who plays it."

Whether or not one is talented or intelligent has nothing to do with his righteousness before God. Each one is dependent upon Christ who works in and through him. Only the Master's touch makes the difference!

The righteousness Jesus speaks of includes justification and sanctification. The hungering and thirsting for righteousness is the ultimate desire to be free from sin and its dominion. Lloyd-Jones writes, "It means a desire to be free from the very desire for sin, because we find that the man who truly examines himself in the light of the Scriptures not only discoveres that he is in bondage of sin; still more horrible is the fact that he likes it, that he wants it. Even after he has seen it is wrong, he still wants it. But now the man who hungers and thirsts after righteousness is a man who wants to get rid of that desire for sin, not only outside, but inside as well. In other words, he longs for deliverance from . . . the pollution of sin. Sin is something that pollutes the very essence of our being and of our nature. The Christian is one who desires to be free from all that."[3]

The desire to be holy is to long to be like Christ, the new man in Christ Jesus.

II

The Christian Has a Deep Yearning to Be All that God Wants Him to Be

God knows the secret longing of the heart. He judges one by his dreams—his deep yearning to be what God wants. In spite of failures and shortcomings, God looks upon the heart. He knows the real motives and the dreams that push men along.

This deep yearning is expressed by Jesus as a hungering and thirsting for righteousness. Perhaps this is a reflection from Jesus' recent experience of fasting 40 days and nights in the wilderness during His period of temptation. The agony of hungering and thirsting was still vivid in His memory. But with that background, He says that's how men should crave and desire God's righteousness in their lives. He asks, "How much do you want goodness? Do you want it as much as a starving man wants food, and as much as a man dying of thirst wants water?" If one desires God's righteousness like that, what a difference it will make in his life!

Certain things stand out when Jesus puts it like hungering and thirsting.

Hungering and thirsting are signs of health. One of the earliest signs of life in a normal baby is hunger. This first instinct of the newly born infant is a sign of health. Whenever the appetite is absent, it is a sign of disease or sickness. The person who does not hunger and thirst for what God wants him to be must reasonably conclude that his soul is in an unhealthy, unnatural condition. He is spiritually sick—and thus needs an appointment with the Great Physician. One who is truly born again will experience a "hunger and thirst after righteousness."

Hungering and thirsting are signs of dependence on outside nourishment. The body cannot live on itself for long. The nourishment must come from beyond the body. A lady gave me a plaque that hangs on the wall of my study. It says, "Man cannot live by bread alone—it takes peanut butter and jelly, too!" Food must come from outside one's self. It is true of the soul also. The soul cannot be self-supporting, self-subsisting. It cannot live upon itself any more than the body can. Jesus Christ alone is the Bread of Life and the Living Water. He is our Nourisher and Sustainer. The Psalmist sang, "As the hart [deer] panteth after the water brooks, so panteth my soul after thee, O God. My soul thirsteth for God, for the living God" (Ps. 42:1-2).

Hungering and thirsting are signs of desperation. Since hunger unsatisfied leads to death, there is a desperation, an agony for that which can sustain life. There is a compelling quality in thirst that is unequalled. When the soul really thirsts for God, his cup can be filled to overflowing.

Many years ago, I travelled with my parents in a slow-moving, Model A Ford from California to Denver, Colo. The word *eternity* has a special meaning for each person, but my definition of *eternity* is a trip through the Great American Desert of the Southwest in an un-air-conditioned Model A—and back! One miserable, hot afternoon on the return journey, we were driving along the Colorado

River. The hot desert wind was like a blast from hell's furnace. I was so thirsty I couldn't see anything but that river of cool, refreshing water. By the time we reached a gasoline station in Needles, I was nearly driven mad by the thought of a drink of water. Before Dad turned the engine off, I burst out of the door and ran to the drinking fountain. The first mouthful passed before I had a chance to taste it, but the second lodged on top of my tongue! I had to spit it out. That was one of the greatest shocks and disappointments of my childhood days. The water was full of sulphur. It even smelled like rotten eggs!

My yearning for water was not satisfied, but in our quest for the Living Water there is sure satisfaction. There is a deep and profound yearning within that presses on until it is satisfied in Him. More than passing feeling, it is a compelling desire to know God—not just about Him. One will never know God in His fulness until He becomes our deepest desire.

The *Amplified Bible* says, "Blessed and fortunate and happy and spiritually prosperous (that is, in that state in which the born-again child of God enjoys His favor and salvation) are those who hunger and thirst for righteousness (uprightness and right standing with God), for they shall be completely satisfied!" (Matt. 5:6).

This yearning is for God's righteousness—all of it, the whole thing! In ordinary conversational Greek, when one would speak of being hungry or thirsty, he would use the genitive case, the English equivalent using the word *of.* It would be like this: "I hunger for of the bread." The meaning is that he was hungry for part of the bread—not the whole loaf. The Greek would say, "I thirst for the water." He was saying, "I am thirsty for some of the water—not the whole tank."

When Jesus spoke the fourth beatitude, however, He did not use the usual genitive form, but another known as the accusative. The meaning, then, of this beatitude is not "to hunger or thirst for part of God's righteousness." The accusative that Jesus used means "I hunger and thirst for the whole thing—all of God's righteousness." To say one hungers for bread in the accusative means "I want the whole loaf." To say one thirsts for water in the accusative means "I want the whole pitcherful."[4]

Most people seem to be content with a part of goodness and righteousness—the parts they like best. It is not enough to be satisfied with partial goodness. It must be total and complete. One could translate Jesus' words, "Blessed are those who hunger and thirst for the whole of righteousness, for total righteousness, for complete righteousness."[5]

Yearning for all of God's righteousness is the Christian's way of life. Hungering and thirsting is not confined to a few moments at church or when someone dies!

For example, this kind of hungering and thirsting for righteousness ought to make a man live better, not just get him ready to die. While we like to have God's blessing, we must also accept His way. Balaam, the false prophet, was being tempted to ungodliness and an unholy allegiance for money and prestige, but he said, "Let me die the death of the righteous, and let my last end be like his!" (Num. 23: 10). Balaam wanted to die like the righteous, but apparently he did not want to live like the righteous.

If one hungers and thirsts for righteousness, he will avoid the things that are bad and harmful to his relationship with God. He will also avoid the things that dull his spiritual appetite.

If one hungers and thirsts for righteousness, it will be a part of his daily concern and call for whatever investment is necessary to achieve it. One's life must be disciplined to receive as God directs. If a man says to himself, "I'm so busy, I don't have time for the quest of spiritual things," then it must be added, "If I am hungering and thirsting after God's righteousness, I will find time." A man who is desperately thirsty for a glass of water, will find time to get what available water is near. It is amazing how people find time to do the things they want to do in all areas of life.

A certain pastor enjoyed the hymn "Take Time to Be Holy." But occasionally he would have his congregation change the words to sing, "Take time to behold Him." That's the secret.

If one is hungering and thirsting after righteousness, he will always put himself in the place of getting it. He will not avoid the places and people in whose presence this filling seems to take place.

Bartimaeus was a blind man. He couldn't heal himself. Do what he could, he could not get back his sight. But Bartimaeus did go and set himself in the place to get it. He heard that Jesus was coming through town, so he went to the highway entering the village. He got as near as he could to where Jesus was passing by. He could not give himself sight, but he could put himself where it was going to be available. Jesus came and gave him his sight.

The man who hungers and thirsts after righteousness knows the crowd where spiritual things like that happen, the group among whom Jesus is found. He will never miss an opportunity to be where people seem to find the righteousness of God. Uncle Bud Robinson used to speak of "staying under the spout where the glory comes out!"

III

The Christian Can Know and Experience the Joy of Satisfaction

Such a hunger implies that God has something that can and will satisfy the longing of the heart. God has given man a spiritual appetite, and He has made provision to satisfy it.

The promise of Christ in this fourth beatitude is that they who hunger and thirst after righteousness shall be filled. The Greek word for "be filled" comes from a Greek word that usually is translated "grass." In other words, Jesus is saying that those who hunger and thirst after righteousness shall be like sheep who have grazed until they have eaten themselves clear full. The verb means "satisfied!"

In our spiritual quest, this fulness is God's answer to the emptiness of man's heart.

"Spiritually prosperous are those hungering and thirsting for righteousness, because they themselves shall be filled so as to be completely satisfied" (Matt. 5:6, Wuest).

When the prodigal son was hungry, he went to feed upon the husks of the pigpen, but when he was desperately hungry—starving—he went to his father! Our Heavenly Father can fill the empty void with all the fullness of Christ. John wrote, "And of his fulness have all we received, and grace for grace" (John 1:16).

The joy of the Christian life is a by-product of being filled with God's righteousness. One never finds real happiness and blessing apart from being filled and satisfied by God's righteousness.

Everyone wants to be happy. The quest for happiness is the driving force for most of man's actions, but sadly he can't find happiness by going to look for it. The Bible underscores the fact that real happiness is always a by-product of seeking something else. Righteousness must always come before happiness. Only those who seek righteousness ever experience lasting happiness and joy.

A lot of people spend their lives seeking something they can never find. They go from meeting to meeting, from convention to convention, from specialist to specialist, always hoping to get an experience that will fill them with joy. They see others get it, and they covet it—but they never get it.

"We are not meant to hunger and thirst after experiences; we are not meant to hunger and thirst after blessedness. If we want to be truly happy and blessed, we must hunger and thirst after righteousness. . . . that [happiness] is something that God gives to those who seek righteousness."[6] The fulfillment of righteousness is the secret to happiness.

Clara Teare caught the spirit of the fourth beatitude when she wrote:

All my lifelong I had panted
For a draught from some cool spring
That I hoped would quench the burning
Of the thirst I felt within.

Feeding on the husks around me
Till my strength was almost gone,
Longed my soul for something better,
Only still to hunger on.

Poor I was, and sought for riches,
Something that would satisfy;
But the dust I gathered round me
Only mocked my soul's sad cry.

Well of water, ever springing,
Bread of life, so rich and free,
Untold wealth that never faileth,
My Redeemer is to me.

Hallelujah! I have found Him—
Whom my soul so long has craved!
Jesus satisfies my longings;
Through His blood I now am saved.

6

The Fifth Beatitude

Matthew 5:7

The World Needs Love

On a cassette tape I bought recently, the Boston Pops Orchestra has recorded the beautiful score of a recently popular song. Its melodic line is singable and the harmony is pleasant, but the title is particularly intriguing. For the musical world to enjoy, Arthur Fiedler has captured the enchanting thought, "What the World Needs Now Is Love."

Our poor world has always been in desperate need of real love. That search is not new. I was surprised to learn from Ripley's *Believe It or Not* that in the Lys Valley of France, a stream flows around a stone that is shaped like a heart. Centuries ago people bottled up the water that flowed around the stone heart with the belief that it would assure a loved one's affection. But love is not something one may store in a bottle.

If ever the world needed love, it is now. There are many lonely and unloved people. Dr. Clyde Narramore told of a teacher who worked with mentally retarded children. In the course of his duties, he visited the class and noted that the teacher was outstanding. Often he complimented her for her work, and she showed deep appreciation for his kind words. At the close of the school year, the woman said to Dr. Narramore, "I want to thank you for the encouragement you have given me this year." Then, with tears in her eyes, she added, "You may not believe it, Dr. Narramore, but as a child no one ever showed me much kindness. There was no one to love me. And I was grown before anyone ever told me that he or she cared for me. In fact, I often wondered whether I was worthy of notice or attention. It has bothered me all my life. That's why your encouragement has meant so much to me."[1]

The key to most hearts is love. That's what the world needs now! Jesus, our Contemporary, said, "Blessed are the merciful: for they shall obtain mercy" (Matt. 5:7). He speaks to a world that clamors for its rights, that is embedded in the "me first" philosophy and that demonstrates that might makes right.

In the fifth beatitude, Jesus comes to a turning point. In the first four beatitudes, He talks about the Christian in terms of his spiritual need. But now Jesus deals with the Christian's disposition and relationships to others, which necessarily are altered by the impact of the first four beatitudes. As one's spiritual needs are being met, he is changed by God's ministry in his life. The Christian must live differently. His disposition must be purified by Christ.

The tragedy of the Christian faith is that so many verbal adherents are clumsy boors that think they must speak their mind frankly. Some have developed a critical, harsh, judgmental attitude and are the world's worst advertisement for any religion! One little girl had apparently come across a few of these "ultraright" people. She prayed, "O Lord, make all the bad people good and the good people nice."

Jesus tempers a Christian's knowledge and desire for

rightness and justice with these words: "Blessed are the merciful: for they shall obtain mercy." That is love in action!

I

Mercy Is an Active Kindness

The Jewish people who first heard Jesus say, "Blessed are the merciful," had codified mercy into two acts; (1) giving pardon for an injury, and (2) giving alms to the poor. But we have almost narrowed it to forgiveness for wrongdoing. This negative idea means little more than "I won't punish you if you won't punish me!"

However, Jesus inserts one of the great Old Testament ideas into the Sermon on the Mount. The Hebrew word *chesed,* translated generally "mercy," is used more than 150 times. In the Old Testament it is much broader than simply remission of a penalty or relaxing some demand. *Chesed* is more positive. At least 38 times in the KJV it is translated as "kindness." Our present English word *kindness* really seems to carry the Hebrew thought and Jesus' usage much better than our modern English word *mercy.* When *chesed* is used of God, it describes His outgoing kindness. It is the basis of God's whole relationship to man. Many, many times in the Old Testament, *chesed* described God's covenant with Israel.

When Jesus was speaking of "mercy," He did not suggest one should sit back and do nothing, waiting for a chance to forgive someone for a wrongdoing. But this kind of mercy is an attitude that rolls up its sleeves and looks for ways to extend a helping hand. Kindness is service, love in action!

Allan Knight Chalmers wrote the book *High Wind at Noon.* In it is a character named Peter Holm. After a career as a famous engineer, building bridges, tunnels, railroads, he came to a period of destitution. Back to his hometown he came with his wife and daughter. Peter lived in poverty and sickness.

A neighboring farmer had a vicious dog that had frightened the community. In spite of warnings that the dog was dangerous, the old farmer gave no heed. One day Peter Holm came home to find the dog mauling the lifeless body of his little girl. The sheriff came and shot the killer dog. The neighbors all turned against the old farmer whom they held responsible for the tragedy. No one would sell him grain for his fields when the time for sowing came. They wouldn't speak to the old man. The poor man was desperate.

One night Peter could not sleep for thinking about his neighbor. Finally he got up, went to his shed, and took his last bushel of barley. Peter sowed the grain in the man's plowed but bare field. To everyone's surprise, when the seeds came up, it was obvious what Peter had done—for part of his own field was bare, while the field of his neighbor was green.[2]

That is mercy—love in action! While it is not easy, it flows from a heart where Christ really lives!

This kind of mercy deals also in trifles, in the little things that people experience every day.

President Abraham Lincoln had received guests at a state dinner in the White House. When some friends from his hometown came to visit, the rough frontiersmen were invited to stay for the meal. The politicians and backwoods people were seated together around the fancy table.

During the formal meal, one of the country fellows poured his coffee into his saucer and blew on it to cool it. As was his custom, the man sipped enthusiastically from the saucer.

Lincoln saw the highbrows grinning at each other with disdain. They silently watched to see the president's reaction. Unceremoniously Lincoln poured his cup of coffee into the saucer, blew on it, and sipped from his saucer. Interestingly, all the guests followed suit.

The people who intend to follow Jesus Christ will develop a sensitivity for the feelings of others. They will act to help, to share another's shame, to ease the hurts and burdens of others. One man wrote, "Kindness is a language the dumb can speak and the deaf can hear and understand."

II

Mercy Is a Godlike Quality

Some 9 out of 10 of the Old Testament references to the word *mercy* have to do with God and the actions of God. The Bible tells us over and over that God delights in mercy. Another oft-repeated statement is that His "mercy endureth for ever"—for example, in each of the 26 verses of Psalm 136. Mercy, or active kindness, is an attribute of God's nature.

The prophet Micah says, "He hath shewed thee, O man, what is good; and what doth the Lord require of thee, but to do justly, and to love mercy, and to walk humbly with thy God?" (Micah 6:8). This Godlike quality is required in men. Jesus added, "Be merciful, just as your Father is merciful" (Luke 6:36, NIV). The man of God is to evidence this kindness in his life. Someone has written, "Nowhere do we imitate God more than in showing mercy." God expects this mercy or active kindness to be characteristic of a Christian's relationship with others. The man who fails to display this Godlike trait is condemned by the Word of God. Clement of Alexandria spoke of the merciful man as one who "practices being God"!

Unfortunately this is the quality sadly lacking in some who make a religious profession. They make rigid demands on other people's conduct and pass judgment on other persons' motives, but fail to take any positive action to help someone the day after Sunday. Lack of mercy is an unlovely, sour thing.

A church committee went to the railway station to greet their new pastor. None of them had ever seen him before. As they watched each passenger get off the train, they tried to see if they could guess which one was the minister. Finally they walked up to a man and asked him, "Are you our new Christian leader?"

Rather surprised, he replied, "No, I am not. I have a sour stomach, and that's what makes me look this way."

Outward righteousness without mercy gives a man indigestion of the disposition. Dr. E. Stanley Jones said, "But nothing is more beautiful than the countenance of righteousness when there glistens upon it the tear of mercy."[3]

If one's religion makes him a hard, stern, unsympathetic critic, he has missed the Christlike quality that always goes with the Christ-filled, Christ-controlled life.

A group of college professors met to discuss disciplinary procedures for the misconduct of several students. The name of one young student came up, and one professor insisted on a severe punishment. He judiciously pointed out that they couldn't just pretend the rules had not been broken. Then he added, "After all, God has given us eyes."

"Yes," replied another professor, "but He also gave us eyelids."

To understand the nature of mercy, one may look at the Latin word *misericordia,* from which comes the English word *mercy*. It is the combination of two words, *miserans,* "pity" or "pain," and *cordia,* "the heart." Mercy means "pain of heart." If we would be merciful to men with the same attitude that God has, we must learn to think toward men as God does, to feel for them as God feels for them, to act toward men as God acts toward them.

III

Mercy Sets the Climate for Spiritual Change

A few years ago I discovered for myself a principle of human relations. For best results, never force a man to defend himself. For example, a man states that he has done something, and I react by saying, "That's not right. You should not do that!" I have merely forced him to back up his actions. If he has a normal, well-balanced personality, he will try to defend himself—even if he knows he is wrong. By my refusal to accept him, I force him into a corner to defend something that he doesn't really want to defend.

If, instead, I would listen and accept what he said with love, attempting to understand, I have given him an opportunity to change his mind or change his course of action. He does not lose face by changing to a better position. I have created the climate for easy change.

By forgiving someone, we really set him free. We do not have to approve the wrongdoing or unkindness, but there is no point in crushing the sinner just to condemn the sin. Forgiveness and mercy, acts of kindness, enable the other fellow to change his behavior and attitude.

Augsburger put it well:

> When a person sins against you and then asks forgiveness, if you first make him crawl before you and then say he is forgiven, the truth is that you have not really forgiven him. What you did was to punish him emotionally, to balance your emotional ledger, and then say, "Now we can forget it." To forgive is actually to free the other person from recrimination or judgment, leaving the door open for the reconciliation and the "healing" of the situation.[4]

One should forget his personal resentment and thus by

God's grace create the atmosphere of love. In that climate, men make remarkable changes in the moral and spiritual realm.

Frederick William Faber wrote:

> Kind words are the music of the world. They have the power which seems to be beyond natural causes, as if they were some angels' song which had lost its way and came on earth. It seems as if they could almost do what in reality God alone can do—soften the hard and angry hearts of men. No one was ever corrected by a sarcasm—crushed, perhaps, if the sarcasm was clever enough, but drawn to God, never.[5]

Wherever and whenever people are suffering, the Christian is faced with a claim on his life. Dietrich Bonhoeffer, martyr in a Nazi prison, described the merciful Christians:

> They have an irresistible love for the down-trodden, the sick, the wretched, the wronged, the outcast and all who are tortured with anxiety. They go out and seek all who are enmeshed in the toils of sin and guilt. No distress is too great, no sin too appalling for their pity. If any man falls into disgrace, the merciful will sacrifice their own honour to shield him, and take his shame upon themselves.[6]

This mercy or active kindness, this outgoing love, deliberately chooses to identify with the sufferings of others.

Aarlie J. Hull gave a condensation in the *Herald of Holiness* magazine of a speech by a very close personal friend, Ruth Croft Weber. As Ruth told this story from her own experience, there unfolded a classic example of mercy, of Christian kindness and love. Here are Ruth's words:

"My mother was a social worker and a few years ago called me from her office to see if I would help care for a lady who was very ill with cancer. The strange thing about this case was that the woman had not let another human being inside her house for two years.

"The first day I was supposed to go, Mother called to

say that a visiting nurse had been there and found that the reason she wouldn't let anyone in her house was because there was a dead dog on the foot of the bed under the bedclothes. Detailed records showed that the animal, her only friend, had died two years before.

"I drove to her house with some apprehension. I turned into a long driveway that led to the shack which had been her prison for two whole years. I entered the kitchen.

"I have never seen or smelled such squalor. Ahead of me was the bedroom and a small, lightless bathroom. The walls were grimy with grease and cobwebs. The only two windows were pasted with layers of newspaper. The floor was filthy. As I walked past the stove, I lifted a lid off a pan and the stench was awful!

"Then I saw her—the most emaciated, pitiful human being I have ever seen! Beside her on the bed was a fat purse, which I soon learned I was to stay away from.

"As I looked at Madonna Briggs, my heart reached out to her. I forgot about the dead dog, the filth, and the odor.

"I quickly proceeded to meet her needs, making dumb conversation about the weather or whatever was at hand. . . .

"As we talked, I literally dug into the cleaning. . . .

"On my second or third visit, she started giving orders. I was delighted! It was a spark of humanity revived.

"My days with Mrs. Briggs were spent scrubbing and picking up, emptying her ashtrays, bringing her pills, lifting her to the bathroom, urging her to take one more bite of food, and being careful not to get near that purse.

"One day I was dressing her for a visit to the doctor. I sat beside her on the bed, pulled a stocking on her incredibly thin leg, looked into her face, and said, 'Mrs. Briggs, God loves you.' Before she had a chance to stop me, I was telling her about what Jesus had done for me, about the joy and peace I knew through Him. She changed the subject. But I told her the plan of salvation again . . . again . . . and again. I could, you see, because *I had earned the right to witness to her.*

"On Friday, I stopped by with a piece of cake, and we visited and even laughed a bit together. The next day she died. . . .

"We are all surrounded by people, but how many have we loved? Really loved! Do we listen? Do we look past the words they are saying to the cry of their hearts? Do we love unconditionally as God loves us?"[7]

Jesus knows that people respond to love. That's what our world needs now. "Blessed are the merciful: for they shall obtain mercy."

St. Francis of Assissi summed it up in his famous prayer:

"Lord, make me an instrument of Thy peace; where there is hatred, let me sow love; where there is injury, pardon; where there is doubt, faith; where there is despair, hope; where there is darkness, light; and where there is sadness, joy.

"O Divine Master, grant that I may not so much seek to be consoled, as to console; to be understood, as to understand; to be loved, as to love; for it is in giving that we receive; it is in pardoning that we are pardoned, and it is in dying that we are born to eternal life."

7 / The Sixth Beatitude

Matthew 5:8

Cleanliness Is Godliness

Mothers try in desperation to teach young boys the extrabiblical proverb, "Cleanliness is next to godliness." However, Bishop J. Paul Taylor suggests that in the spiritual world "cleanliness *is* godliness." Jesus said to His disciples, "Blessed are the pure in heart: for they shall see God" (Matt. 5:8). Christ underscored the truth that purity is God's plan for Christian living.

A man in Tibet was performing his religious rites when two tourists came along. They noticed that the old man was unkempt, forgetting that he lived in a primitive environment. Unaware that the old priest could speak their language, the travelers talked between themselves of his appearance. When the man finished his religious ritual, he smiled at the visitors and said, "But my heart is clean!"

Men become adept at judging one's outward appearance, but God looks on the heart. He knows the masquerader and the one who is truly "pure in heart." The Word of

God confirms that "cleanliness is godliness" in the realm of the spirit.

Every department store has its bargain counters. Good quality merchandise is reduced in price for one reason or another. Delight brightens the eyes of the shopper to find such wonderful items for such cheap prices. But if one looks closely, the truth may be revealed. A little, inconspicuous sign will say, "Slightly soiled, greatly reduced in price."

Charles Koller comments:

> In the market of life we find much human material similarly marked down. Many of these people are gifted, cultured, and of high potential, but slightly soiled—in speech, in character, in reputation—and drastically reduced in worth. They are not ruined; but they are disqualified for the highest achievements; they are defeated in their noblest aspirations. The best to which they can ever attain is only second best to that which might have been, had they kept their hands clean and their hearts pure.[1]

In contrast, Jesus says, "Happy are those whose hearts are pure, for they shall see God" (Matt. 5:8, TLB). True godliness lies in purity of the heart. God desires to wash away wickedness and impurity. He can leave the soul unmuddied.

A glass of water may look pure and clean, but if when it is shaken, the water becomes clouded, it is obvious that the impurities have not been taken out. However, when the same glass of water is filtered until all the filth, dirt, and impurities are removed, then no amount of disturbance will cloud the water. It is pure and clean. God is not only willing to forgive our sins, the expressions of our soiled souls, but God is also faithful "to cleanse us from all unrighteousness" (1 John 1:9). He provides a cleansing from impurity.

Cleanliness is godliness; godliness is purity!

I

Purity—What Is It?

Jesus is speaking of a pure, cleansed heart or life.

In the New Testament there are three Greek words for "purity." *Hagnos,* where we get our word for "holy," means "pure from defilement, not contaminated." A second Greek word, *eilikrines,* means "unalloyed, unmixed substances." In the New Testament it is used to describe Christian morality and ethics, with the idea of "sincerity." It meant literally "tested by the sunlight." The object could be held up to the sunlight, and one would know if it were pure, clear, and unmixed. Many people these days speak of being "transparent," meaning open, clear character, sincere, pure motives.

In this sixth beatitude, Jesus used another Greek word, *katharos,* from whence we get our English word *catharsis,* or a cleansing process. Hence this verse has been translated, "Happy are the clean in heart." Thus, purity of heart is the result of a soul being cleansed by the grace of God, not simply undergoing a religious purification ceremony. The word *pure* or catharsis was originally used to describe soiled clothes that have been washed clean clear through. Never could this word be used to describe a Christian who was partially soiled—living by faith, but sinning along the way! It is a contradiction in terms.

The cleansed life is evidenced by a single-mindedness or sincerity of purpose. The life is empty of hypocrisy or playacting. Jesus said later in the Sermon on the Mount, "If therefore thine eye be single, thy whole body shall be full of light. But if thine eye be evil, thy whole body shall be full of darkness" (Matt. 6:22-23). Purity of heart is singleness of mind or purpose. "It means, if you like, 'without folds;' it is open, nothing hidden. You can describe it as sincerity; it means single-minded, or single-eyed devotion."[2]

Paul expressed the divided mind, the heart with mixed motives, in his letter to the Romans: "For I delight in the law of God after the inward man; but I see another law in my members, warring against the law of my mind, and bringing me into captivity to the law of sin which is in my members" (Rom. 7:22-23). However, the pure in heart is one who is no longer divided. His first loyalty is to God. He pledges his allegiance inwardly and outwardly to Christ and His righteousness. As Dr. Tasker says: "The pure in heart are the singleminded who are free from the tyranny of a divided self, and who do not try to serve God and the world at the same time."[3]

To be pure in heart is to have an undivided love in keeping the first and great commandment, "Thou shalt love the Lord thy God with all thy heart, and with all thy soul, and with all thy mind" (Matt. 22:37).

II

Purity—for Whom?

Jesus addressed these words to His disciples—those who had forsaken all to follow Christ. Every born-again Christian is eligible for heart purity. The man living for Christ in this polluted world can come to a point of full surrender to Jesus. The Master anxiously awaits to take possession and control of the throne of his heart.

Absolutely no one is naturally pure in heart. The finer things of life, like education and culture, cannot transform the nature of a man's soul. Hearts can be made pure only by a work of divine grace. Every person who has his sins forgiven is a candidate for the sixth beatitude, "Blessed are the pure in heart"!

Many people have rebelled against the old "puritanism" because it went to ridiculous extremes. Its greater fault was its emphasis on "external purity." Purity of life must come from within. Jesus Christ offers a pure heart to His disciples because without it there can be no pure living. In the soul cleanliness is godliness. One's outward life reflects his inner nature. When the Psalmist asks who can stand in God's holy presence, the answer comes, "He that hath clean hands, and a pure heart" (Ps. 24:4). The clean hands cannot be separated from the pure heart. Clean actions spring from a cleansed life.

William Barclay told of the Danish sculptor Thorwaldsen. He had completed a famous statue of Jesus, and its fame spread over Europe. One day the French government offered him a commission at a high salary to carve the statue of the Roman goddess Venus. He answered, "The hands which carved the figure of Christ can never carve the figure of a heathen goddess."[4]

The reason the pure in heart can be happy is that, having been cleansed through Christ's atonement, they can live pure and clean lives!

III

Purity—Where?

Jesus said, "Blessed are the pure in heart"! He did not ascribe perfection in actions or judgment, but He spoke of purity in the areas of desires and affections.

W. E. McCumber put it well:

> Anyone who studies the Old Testament usage of "heart" . . . will be amazed at the number of times it occurs and the variety of meanings it has. Of course the ancient writers knew the heart as a physical organ. And because emotional reactions were accompanied by felt changes in the rate and rhythm of pulsation, "heart" was used to describe the emotional activities. But it was employed far more frequently with the activities of the

> intellect and the will. Its connection with the intellectual and volitional processes is what gives "heart" its "distinctive stamp in Hebrew thought." . . . In short, the heart stood for the entire inner life, the capacity and energy of a person to feel, think, and resolve, with emphasis on the thinking and willing.[5]

In Semitic speech, heart includes the mind as well as the emotions.

This is brought out in the translation which reads, "How fortunate are those with pure minds." One man said, "Cleanse the fountain if you would purify the streams." If one wishes to live without guilt, he must not try to ignore it. He must not try to lower his standards to meet his conduct. A man must let Christ cleanse his heart and mind so he can change his conduct and live above guilt! The prayer of the Psalmist expresses it well: "Create in me a new, clean heart, O God, filled with clean thoughts and right desires" (Ps. 51:10, TLB).

IV

Purity—When?

God's offer of a pure heart is here and now—in this present life. Unfortunately many people think death brings their only moment of freedom from impurity and sin's dominion. But death brings no moral attribute with it at all. Some believe that to live a cleansed life they must retreat from the real world. Purity of heart is to will one will with God in this present life.

Jesus came to earth and took the form of man. John wrote, "And the Word was made flesh, and dwelt among us" (John 1:14). Christ did not retreat from life, from sinful men, from the pressures of an ungodly world. Nor did He design for Christians to run away in seclusion. The Lord knew that the pure in heart could live in the world but be not of the world. In fact, He said in His intercessory prayer, "I pray not that thou shouldest take them out of the world, but that thou shouldest keep them from the evil" (John 17:15).

Myron Augsburger pointed out: "Humanness and sinfulness are not synonymous. God created a good world. God could become man in the Incarnation without being sinful. We can be disciples and live Christlike lives now in this physical body."[6] Christ is our Sovereign in this present life. The body is His temple, not a fun house! Therefore, our pleasures should flow from a cleansed life.

A man was visiting a coal-mining town. To his surprise he noticed a beautiful white flower growing up beside the black, dirty roadway to the mine. The tourist asked a miner, "How can such a pure and beautiful flower be here in these dirty surroundings?"

The miner replied, "Throw some of the coal dust on it and see."

The man did so and noticed that when the dirt touched the white petals of the flower, it slid right off to the ground. The flower was just as lovely as before. It was so smooth that the dirt could not stick to the flower.

Christians cannot avoid living in a world filled with sin and moral pollution. But God can keep them so pure and clean that though they encounter sin on every side, it will not soil their souls. Jesus' disciples can stand in the midst of a dirty world, unsullied by it. "Happy are those whose hearts are pure!" (Matt. 5:8, TLB).

V

Purity—How?

The Bible says, "And God, which knoweth the hearts, bare them witness, giving them the Holy Ghost, even as he did unto us; and put no difference between us and them, purifying their hearts by faith" (Acts 15:8-9). God gave the

Holy Spirit to the Christians to be the purifying or cleansing Agent. He purifies the heart in response to faith—faith that says, "I believe God can, will, and does cleanse me now!"

Paul wrote of Christ, "Who gave himself for us, that he might redeem us from all iniquity, and purify unto himself a peculiar [unique] people, zealous of good works" (Titus 2:14). Christ's atonement is intended to bring to His people a purity of heart and life. This purity is evidenced by good works—works that are morally and ethically good. It is the natural outflow of a cleansed life.

Most Christians have in essence prayed, "Create in me a clean heart, O God, and renew a right spirit within me" (Ps. 51:10). Happily God has not mocked our hopes for purity! God can cleanse my life when I ask Him to take the presidency of my soul. By faith I trust that He will do what He has promised. In response to my faith and my trust in God's Word, the Holy Spirit can and will cleanse my heart from all unrighteousness. That is the gift of the Holy Spirit from God to me—because I need Him.

Man's reaction to impurity is to kill or destroy, but God's reaction to impurity is to cleanse and purify! The pure in heart are blessed and happy because this is the state in which God has designed for us to live. At last we can be our real selves, no longer bent and twisted by sin. The homesickness of the soul is now allayed because the cleansed life is the true homeland of the soul.

The Holy Spirit does not clean me up and run away to heaven to watch to see if I can stay spotless spiritually. Not at all! He comes to do a divine work of grace in me, cleansing this temple for *himself,* for His use. When the Holy Spirit is at home in me, I am at home with God!

J. Sidlow Baxter wrote:

> The Christian life was never meant to be an everlasting "penitent form," a continual returning of the

> prodigal from the far country, an incessant repetition of the publican's groan, "God be merciful to me a sinner". . . . We are no longer merely perpetual petitioners for pardon. We have found the "everlasting mercy" and the blood-bought "forgiveness" which covers all our sin. . . . We are no longer prodigals, we are *at home,* restored to true sonship, and in . . . fellowship with (our Father).[7]

"Blessed are the pure in heart: for they shall see God." John added these words to the record: "Yes, dear friends, we are already God's children, right now, and we can't even imagine what it is going to be like later on. But we do know this, that when he comes we will be like him, as a result of seeing him as he really is" (1 John 3:2, TLB).

8

The Seventh Beatitude

Matthew 5:9

The Mission of Christ's Ambassadors

Serving on a trial jury recently, I learned a little more about the art of self-defense. The defendant had used a knife against a man who happened to be an instructor of karate and other forms of self-defense. The bar fight ended with a stabbing. The witnesses came and went. The lawyers chipped away at the evidence. Twelve men and women sat in silence, trying desperately to be fair and honest. Our assignment was to judge something we had not seen firsthand.

During the long hours of deliberation, the jurors debated over what constitutes self-defense, and who was acting in self-defense. As I weighed what I had heard, I could not forget the best system of self-defense taught in the Bible. Solomon spelled it out: "A soft answer turneth away wrath" (Prov. 15:1).

The disciple of Jesus becomes Christ's ambassador in our world. The Master would have His men learn this noble art of self-defense. Jesus said, "Blessed are the peacemakers: for they shall be called the children of God" (Matt. 5:9).

There is a Chinese proverb that says, "If you talk with a soft voice, you do not need a thick stick." If a man carries a big stick long enough, he will someday have to use it. But the soft word doesn't create fierce challenges.

Jesus' whole life and ministry underscored peace. The angels announced His birth by singing of peace on earth. His last will and testament was "Peace I leave with you, my peace I give unto you" (John 14:27).

The New Testament is interwoven with the theme of peace. Eighty-eight times the word *peace, eirene,* appears —including every book of the New Testament. Each of the Epistles begins and ends with a prayer for peace! The central meaning of this peace is a healing of the breach between God and man—being reconciled to God. Paul wrote, "And all things are of God, who hath reconciled us to himself by Jesus Christ, and hath given to us the ministry of reconciliation" (2 Cor. 5:18). As disciples of the Master, every Christian should live with the demeanor of reconciliation—as one who is now a friend of God.

We are to be ambassadors for Christ in the world. Our assignment is never passive. It is peace-making, reconciling, bringing persons into new relationships with God and with others. "Blessed are the peacemakers, for they will be called sons of God" (Matt. 5:9, NIV). Before we do our homework on this assignment, there are three important factors for the ambassador of Christ.

I

Christ's Ambassador Must Have Christ's Peace Within Himself

This is the qualification for the ministry of reconciliation. One cannot share what he doesn't have. Before he can enjoy the peace of God, a man must know the God of peace! When there is peace with God, this is a big step toward living peaceably with men. When Jesus said, "Happy are the peacemakers!" it was more than a promise; it was a declaration of fact!

Clement of Alexandria wrote of the blessing on "those who have stilled the incredible battle which goes on in their own souls." With joy Paul testified, "I live; yet not I, but Christ liveth in me" (Gal. 2:20). An ambassador of Christ is a happy man, a "man in whom the contradictions are obliterated, the man whose inner battle has been stilled in the control of Christ. Every man must long for peace in the inner warfare of his own personality and his own soul; and Jesus Christ is the only person who can make that peace."[1] You can never qualify as a peacemaker until you have at least some measure of peace in your own heart. Peace is not the absence of conflict, but the ability to cope with it.

The Hebrew word for peace is *shalom*. While it carries the idea of serenity, prosperity, and happiness, it also describes "right personal relationships; it describes intimacy, fellowship, uninterrupted goodwill between man and man."[2] Therefore, this peace is not just the absence of war and strife, but it is the harmonious relationships both horizontal (with men) and vertical (with God)! One cannot live in discord with God or man and have this kind of peace. Christ's ambassador moves into relationships giving peace from the overflow of his own peace-filled heart. Gerald Vann puts it this way: "You create peace in the home by being yourself at peace; . . . you create joy by being yourself filled with joy. Again and again we come back to the same principle: it is what you are that matters most."[3]

In the novel *Ben Hur,* Judah Ben Hur was a young man filled with hate, bitterness, resentment, revenge. In the story, however, his life is touched by Jesus Christ, and Ben Hur says, "He has taken the sword out of my hand." Colleen Townsend Evans added, "That's exactly what Jesus does when He comes into our lives. He takes the swords out of our hands. We no longer want to hurt . . . we want to heal. With His love in our hearts, we shall be able to make peace."[4]

II

Christ's Ambassador Is Committed to Action to Bring About Peace

Here is the vocation of the ministry of reconciliation. The *Amplified Bible* translates the seventh beatitude: "Spiritually prosperous . . . are the makers and maintainers of peace." To be a lover and maker of peace is the vocation of every Christian. Jesus informs His disciples that they must not only *have* peace but *make* it.

Those who are blessed are not just peace-lovers, but peacemakers. Peacemaking is a positive, active vocation—not passive. Christ's ambassador is committed to actively set things at peace. There is no room in this beatitude for spectators. All are cast into the arena who intend to emerge as the King's men!

We aren't called to keep peace like a policeman whose fierce visage and black, shining equipment frightens people into abstaining from conflict. We are called to make peace like a representative of the King of Kings and Lord of Lords! "The inner peace Jesus gives us equips us to go out into the world and bring its warring forces together."[5]

If one would take the name of Christ, he must begin the processes of training himself to live for Christ in his world. No government would pick a man for its ambassador who was haphazard, undisciplined, and crude. The best interests of the nation are served when men are sent who have been trained and are sensitive to the countries where they are to be ministers of peace.

Christians must give serious attention as to how they represent Jesus. The ministry of peace is more than positive thinking. It is Christian living. It is life in action! Paul wrote, "Do everything possible, on your part, to live at peace with all men" (Rom. 12:18, TEV). That admonition leaves no room for ducking responsibility. What can one do to be a maker of peace?

First, the peacemaker should take the lead in healing broken relationships with others. When "all is quiet on the western front," it doesn't always mean there is peace. It may just mean that hatred is in repose, maybe grudges smoldering. But that volcano someday will erupt. Is the Christian to sit and wait for his brother to change his mind and seek forgiveness? Not at all. Jesus said, "Therefore, if thou bring thy gift to the altar, and there rememberest that thy brother hath aught against thee; leave there thy gift before the altar, and go thy way; first be reconciled to thy brother, and then come and offer thy gift" (Matt. 5:23-24). The responsibility of bridging the broken friendship is on the Christian!

Martin Luther used to tell the story of two goats that met on a log placed over deep water. The goats couldn't back up, and there wasn't room to fight. After a short conversation, one of them lay down on the narrow bridge and let the other climb over him. If a dumb goat could lay down to bring peace, think what the kneeling Christian could do to make peace!

Second, the peacemaker should be prepared to face the real issue. The peace of which this seventh beatitude speaks is not a phony peace accomplished by temporarily evading the problem. One may be just piling up trouble for the future because he has merely sidestepped the situation. The ambassador of Christ must be prepared to face difficulty, unpleasantness, unpopularity, and trouble in order to make peace. Often it will involve sacrifice.

Third, the peacemaker should be a resilient person. He may have to absorb the emotional attacks or be the sounding board for the deep frustrations of others. "When malicious words and gossip hit him, they go no further. . . . Instead of reverberating in excitement, he is like a great silencing chamber . . . gossip hits him and is absorbed. Yes, he may feel the sting of it, but he doesn't pass it on. He smothers it with forgiveness."[6]

A little girl snuggled up to her mother one night before bedtime. "Mama," she said, "I was a peacemaker today."

"How was that?" asked the mother.

The girl replied, "I heard something, and I didn't tell it!"

Fourth, the peacemaker knows how to play down differences between people and to highlight the similarities, the common joys. The Bible instructs, "Follow peace with all men" (Heb. 12:14). A man must know how to use good sense in dealing with the intricacies of disrupted relationships. He tells his concerns only to the people who can do something about the situations. He operates openly in love, and does not try to work as an anonymous critic.

Two men came to a disagreement over a trivial issue. It resulted in ill will and resentment. The families of the men were also thrown into the senseless conflict.

Finally a friend of both men decided, "I'm going to be a peacemaker and do what I can to heal the breach between my friends."

Going to Mr. Brown, he asked, "What do you think of my friend Mr. Thompson?"

With anger flashing in his face, Brown retorted, "What do I think of Thompson? He is contemptible!"

However, the peacemaker persisted, "But you must admit he is very kind to his family."

Brown settled down a notch. "Well, it's true. He is kind to his family."

The following day the peacemaker called on his other friend, Thompson. "Do you know what Mr. Brown said about you?"

"Are you kidding? I can well imagine the dirty, unkind things he would say about me!"

"Well," said the peacemaker, "he said that you are very kind to your family!"

Thompson said in surprise, "What? Did he say that about me?"

"He sure did. I heard him myself. Now, what do you think of Mr. Brown?"

Thompson recoiled, "I think he is a rascal, a dirty rat!"

"But," said the peacemaker, "you will have to admit that he is an honest man."

Softening slightly, Thompson admitted, "Yes, Brown is an honest man, but what has that got to do with it?"

The next afternoon the peacemaker called on Brown again. "Do you know that Mr. Thompson said that you are a very honest man?"

"You don't mean it," Brown replied.

"I heard him say it with my own ears!"

Soon Brown and Thompson were together, rejoicing in restored fellowship.

The ambassador of Christ will become a peacemaker when he learns to minimize differences and problems, and begins to emphasize solutions. He will get to the root of the problem by working to reconcile men with God. "For as long as men are at odds with God, they are at odds with themselves and with their neighbors."[7] Christ is the remover of barriers in men's lives. We are brothers in Christ. "Happy are those who strive for peace" (Matt. 5:9, TLB).

III

Christ's Ambassador Represents Christ in His World

Here is the glorification of the ministry of reconciliation. What a pronouncement Jesus made: "They shall be called the children of God"! That is the title and acknowledgment given to makers of peace!

As William Barclay points out, "There are people who are always storm centres of trouble and bitterness and strife. Wherever they are they are either involved in quarrels themselves or the cause of quarrels between others. They are troublemakers. . . . Such people are doing the devil's own work."[8]

But there's another group of people—Christ's representatives in this world—who help bridge the gulfs, heal the breaches, bring sweetness and love! "Such people are doing a godlike work, for it is the great purpose of God to bring peace between men and Himself, and between man and man."[9] Sometimes spectators think peacemakers are cowards or sentimentalists, but God refers to them as His children! That is no small claim. When Jesus said that peacemakers "shall be called the children of God," He was making an announcement that they are His special representatives. The phrase "shall be called" is a Hebrew way of saying, "shall receive the status of." In other words, as Moffatt puts it, the peacemakers "will be ranked sons of God."

The Greek New Testament says literally, "sons of God." When the definite article "the" is omitted, it refers to quality or character. Since Hebrew is deficient in adjectives, ideas of description are often expressed by the phrase "son of," followed by some virtue or quality. For example, a man may be a peaceful man. To express it in Hebrew, one would say, "He is the son of peace." In the New Testament, Barnabas was known as the "son of consolation." He was a comforting, consoling man. When Jesus used this phrase, "sons of God," He was especially saying that the peacemaker is Godlike. William Barclay translated this seventh beatitude with this in mind: "Blessed are those who produce right relationships in every sphere of life, for they are doing Godlike work."[10]

In Jesus Christ we have seen God's attitude toward men. We begin to understand His ministry of reconciliation, of making peace on earth, goodwill toward men! God is the God of peace. "He is ever engaged in healing the wounds and reconciling the enmities of the world."[11] The ambassadors of Christ represent in their world the presence and love of a God of peace. As they do their work of reconciliation, "God shall call them his sons" (Matt. 5:9, NEB). In nothing are they more Godlike! They become partners in Christ's work.

Barclay relates a remarkable incident which took place in the early days of the Second World War. A man from southern India, named Sundaram, was preaching the gospel in Burma when the advance armies of Japan captured him and took him to a guard post. All his possessions were taken, and he was bound as a prisoner.

Finally a Japanese officer came in, examined Sundaram's few belongings, and then noticed his Tamil Bible. Though he knew nothing of the Tamil language, he recognized it as a Bible. The officer held it before the missionary prisoner. Upon his hand, the officer traced the sign of the cross and looked at Sundaram.

Sundaram knew nothing of the Japanese language but seemed to understand that the officer was asking if he were a Christian. Sundaram nodded. Barclay concludes the story as follows:

> The officer walked across to him, stood in front of him with his arms stretched out in the form of the Cross, cut his bonds, gave him back his belongings, and

> pointed to the door, bidding him to go. . . . Here were two men who knew not a word of each other's language, two men from nations which were at war, two men between whom there stretched a gulf which was humanly speaking beyond bridging—and Christ bridged that gulf. Jesus Christ reached out across the divisions and in Christ brought two men together again.[12]

Every Christian has been given the glorious privilege of representing Christ in his world. If peacemaking will ever be done seriously, it will come through obedient, sensitive ambassadors of Christ.

Myron S. Augsburger told this story that demonstrates the beauty of this seventh beatitude.

"I recall, as a boy, my father working on a construction job in an apartment complex. After some months he was promoted to foreman, a position another man wanted. For days this man tried various things to turn the men against my father. A part of this was to ridicule some of my father's Christian convictions, especially his commitment to the way of peace and nonviolence.

"Suddenly a slump in work meant that a number of men were laid off, including my father's rival. For a number of days following, when my father went to work, he'd see this man among those at the gate hoping to be given work.

"One day there was need for two more men on one of the jobs, and my father went to the gate to pick two. He looked over the crowd and picked the first carpenter and told him to go to work; then, looking over the rest, he picked out his rival and said, 'Get your tools, Bob, and come to work.' "

Many years later Myron Augsburger encountered his father's old tormentor and rival. When the man discovered who his father was, he responded, "Now, there's a man who lives for God! I saw it in his attitude at work."[13]

"Blessed are the peacemakers: for they shall be called

the children [sons] of God." In word and deed, each Christian needs to stand in for Jesus in his community. Giving himself to this ministry, he may introduce his world to Christ!

9

The Eighth Beatitude

Matthew 5:10-12

Leap for Joy

On his birthday, the little boy's father took him to a pet shop. His choice of a puppy was the number one birthday present. Long minutes passed as the lad eyed each bundle of wriggly fur. Finally he said, "Daddy, I want that one!"

"Which one?" his father asked.

Pointing to a puppy with his tail eagerly wagging, the boy said, "The one with a happy ending."

Jesus finished the eighth and last beatitude with a happy ending. The whole atmosphere of the eighth beatitude is one of joy. Jesus earmarked it with the words: "Rejoice, and be exceeding glad" (Matt. 5:12). While Kingdom living is no easy and comfortable experience, walking with Jesus is not a long-faced, sour, and sad life. In spite of hardships, the Christian can cultivate the habit of happiness by seeing the ups and downs in true perspective. Paul testified, "For our light affliction, which is but for a moment, worketh for us a far more exceeding and eternal weight of glory; while we look not at the things which are seen, but at the things which are not seen: for the things which are seen are temporal; but the things which are not seen are eternal" (2 Cor. 4:17-18).

To Christians facing persecution and insult for Christ's sake, Jesus said, "Rejoice, and be exceeding glad" —or as someone has said, "Rejoice and leap for joy" (Matt. 5:12). While one may be the subject of ridicule by a world that does not understand, down inside he can be so filled with the blessing of God that he leaps for joy!

One morning I put on my coat, picked up my briefcase, told my family "good-bye," and headed for the door to go to work. My dog, Skipper, saw the process taking place. He began to jump up and down, leaping into the air and twirling around. I thought to myself, "That is surely a great display of enthusiasm. He's excited about the idea of going with me." His eagerness broke out into barks of delight as we approached the front door. Skipper gave the best demonstration I ever saw of someone "leaping for joy."

Then all of a sudden, the truth came to me. He is excited because he knows he is *going someplace*. That should excite every born-again Christian, every child of God! Regardless of the bitter circumstances, the severe insults, the pettiness of little minds around us, we are going someplace. We are headed somewhere. Persecution might be our cup of suffering for the moment, but, Christian, leap for joy! We are going home with Jesus someday soon. "Rejoice, and be exceeding glad: for great is your reward in heaven"!

I

Leap for Joy Because God's Man Is Different

God's man is unlike the man who is not a Christian. His values are different. His perspective is different. Paul describes it this way: "For they that are after the flesh do mind the things of the flesh; but they that are after the Spirit the things of the Spirit" (Rom. 8:5).

Many people admire Jesus from a distance, but they have never come to Him personally. If they drew near, and saw what He stands for, they would hate Him just as those men of His day hated Him. Christ doesn't change. The natural man does not change. The popular movements that gather around the name of Jesus have not yet caught the full vision of His imperial claim. The natural man will not applaud Jesus when he sees Him fully.

Martin Lloyd-Jones wrote, "If you try to imitate Christ the world will praise you; if you become Christlike it will hate you."[1] If one is really Christlike, we will not be rewarded with recognition by men. Most likely his reward from men will be rejection because of what and who he is! No longer controlled by the natural self, he is dominated by Jesus Christ. Because of this difference, persecution can arise. The Christian has chosen to live cross-current to the stream of humanity.

There is a disturbing difference between the Christian and the natural man—and people hate to be disturbed. William Barclay stated this problem:

> The Christian does not even need to speak; his presence and his life are a conscience to the sphere, the society, the circle in which he moves. It is not a matter of spoken criticism and constant fault-finding; it is not a matter of conscious superiority, it is simply that the existence of the Christian life is a reminder of what life ought to be and a condemnation of the world as it is. It is no new thing for a man to seek to silence his conscience. The Christian as the conscience of the community must be exposed to the dislike, the hatred, and the attack of that part of the world which lives without God.[2]

Since the Christian has a different nature, he is a different man. The non-Christian recognizes this fundamental difference, and he begins to create friction and to spread twisted rumors to insult.

The Christian ethic, being lofty, becomes a condemnation by simple comparison. People naturally wish to eliminate anyone or anything that condemns them.

Aristides the Just was a famous statesman of ancient Athens, whose life ended in exile. His goodness caused others to be humiliated and ashamed of their own conduct. Finally the citizens called for a vote to banish Aristides the Just. Each citizen was given an ostracon, which was a piece of pottery. If they wished to exile Aristides, they were to write his name on the ostracon.

One illiterate man, who had never seen Aristides, came to vote. Not recognizing Aristides, the ignorant man turned to him and asked him to write the name Aristides on the ostracon for him. He wished to vote to banish the statesman. Curiously, the unrecognized Aristides asked the man, "Has Aristides ever done you any wrong that makes you want to vote for his banishment?"

"None at all," he said. "I don't even know the man. But I am tired of hearing him called 'The Just.'"

One man said to Socrates, "Socrates, I hate you; for when I am with you, I realize what I am."[3]

The child of God can leap for joy because he is different from a self-serving, morally bankrupt world.

II

Leap for Joy Even Though God's Man Will Face Suffering for Christ's Sake

"Blessed are they which are persecuted for righteousness' sake. . . . Blessed are ye, when men shall revile you, and persecute you, and shall say all manner of evil against you falsely, for my sake" (Matt. 5:10-11).

Since men brought lying witnesses to condemn the

Lord himself, the disciple can expect that this might happen to him also. He is not above his master. F. B. Meyer noted, "It is impossible to follow the Lord closely, and not be bespattered by the mud that was cast at Him."[4]

In a letter to Timothy, Paul wrote, "Indeed all who desire to live a godly life in Christ Jesus will be persecuted" (2 Tim. 3:12, RSV). When in verse 10 Jesus speaks of being persecuted for righteousness' sake, He was including all the acts of violence directed toward a Christian. In verse 11 the Master includes all the verbal and emotional abuse that can be heaped upon His man. Though the Christian is dogged by the enemy of his soul or taunted, denounced, and given a bad name, Jesus says, "What happiness will be yours when people blame you and ill-treat you and say all kinds of slanderous things against you for my sake!" (Matt. 5:11, Phillips). Leap for joy! Even in the face of opposition! But why should one rejoice about that?

First, he is making it easier for those who follow him. Pioneers in the faith have always suffered, but as a result less opposition falls on others later. Every freedom we have has been paid for by the suffering of people before us.

Second, persecution is a compliment. As Barclay says, "To persecute a person is to show that we take him so seriously that we consider that he must be eliminated. No one will persecute a person who is futile, ineffective, and indecisive."[5]

Third, one can rejoice in the fact that he is in good company. "For so persecuted they the prophets which were before you" (Matt. 5:12). To suffer for Christ is to share in a great succession.

Fourth, to experience persecution is to have an opportunity to demonstrate loyalty to Jesus Christ. In the second century of the Christian Church, Polycarp, the bishop of Smyrna, was martyred for his faith. His last prayer was, "I thank Thee that Thou hast graciously thought me worthy of this day and of this hour." His crime? He set Christ above Caesar.

Judson was tortured in the prisons of Burma for his Christian faith. After his release he asked the king for permission to preach in a certain Burmese city. The king said, "I am willing for a dozen preachers to go to that city, but not you. Not with those hands. My people are not fools enough to listen to and follow your words, but they will not be able to resist those scarred hands."[6]

In spite of suffering, there can be the joy of conquest for Christ's sake.

III

Leap for Joy Because God's Man Has a Great Tomorrow

"Rejoice, and be exceeding glad: for great is your reward in heaven" (Matt. 5:12). What one sees today is not the end. God's tomorrow is greater yet. In response to persecution of any sort, God's man does not have to be defensive. He can leave the outcome with God.

In Colombia a Christian farmer worked his fields during the week and witnessed for Christ wherever he could. On Sundays he preached in the little village. One day 20 men kidnapped him from his home and took him to a cemetery. They buried him up to his neck in an open grave. Two demands were put to him: first, that he switch political parties; and second, that he renounce his evangelical faith. Since the political issue was not fundamental with him, he agreed to change his political affiliation. But though they threatened to murder him, the humble farmer would not give up his religion. In the face of venomous hate, he prayed, "God, You called me to preach the gospel. If I can win more souls by dying than living, then I am ready to die, Lord."

In a burst of fury one of the men shot the Christian and killed him on the spot. However, the angry mob sobered quickly, for they had witnessed a fearless faith in Christ. Within the month, 15 of the 20 men had turned to the local evangelical congregation and confessed their sins to Jesus Christ. The courage of one of God's men brought many others to Christ.

The bystander might think that the farmer lost the confrontation, but not so. God's tomorrows are rich and full: "For great is your reward in heaven." "There is no assurance of vindication or reward among men now. The reward belongs with certainty to the future."[7] Christ says to His people, "Fear none of those things which thou shalt suffer . . . be thou faithful unto death, and I will give thee a crown of life" (Rev. 2:10). Someone has written, "Christ our Captain has not promised us a smooth voyage across the sea of life, but He has promised us a safe anchorage in the eternal Haven of Rest."

Leap for joy, child of God! You are promised a fantastic tomorrow.

Many years ago a ship pulled into New York Harbor. Brass bands and crowds of people were on hand to welcome Teddy Roosevelt back from an African hunting expedition. Unnoticed by the cheering mobs, a missionary and his wife disembarked from the same ship, returning after many years of sacrificial labor. No one was there to welcome the weary missionary couple. They walked in their loneliness to a cheap hotel.

The contrast seemed to gnaw at the missionary's heart. That night he began to pray about his bitterness and discouragement. "Lord, it just isn't right. A big parade to greet that politician, but no one to welcome us—servants of God. Lord, no one seems to care. We've worked so hard for Thee all our lives, and then when we come home . . ."

God seemed to interrupt him, "But you are not home yet!"

Children of God, we are going somewhere. We seek a better land than this. Leap for joy because He has prepared a place for us for all eternity. We are going home someday, and it will be worth it all!

IV

Leap for Joy Because God's Blessing Can Endure

"Blessed are they which are persecuted . . . Blessed are ye, when men shall revile you . . . Rejoice, and be exceeding glad" (Matt. 5:10-12). Suffering cannot destroy the blessing of God. Persecution cannot stamp out the inner joy. Persecution is not essential to blessedness, but it is compatible with it. All the time Jesus talks about persecution He begins by saying, "Happy are they . . . Happy are ye!" Deep within is a calm joy, but it splashes over and stirs the emotions when needed. The joy of Christ springing up within is more than a theory; it is a wonderful experience and relationship with God. As Barclay puts it, "It is the joy of the climber who has reached the summit, and who leaps for joy that the mountain path is conquered."[8]

God's blessing can endure to the end. The grammatical form of the word "rejoice" means literally "be rejoicing" (Matt. 5:12, Wuest). Christian joy is a continual state. It is not a once-in-a-lifetime experience, but a way of life. As you walk with Christ, regardless of the outward circumstances, be rejoicing! Leap for joy, man of God; you are a born winner! "If God be for us, who can be against us?" (Rom. 8:31).

In Cologne, Germany, there is a cellar where fugitives from the war were hid. Some unknown person carved these words on the wall during the days of agony:

I believe in the sun, even when it is not shining.
I believe in love, even when feeling it not.
I believe in God, even when He is silent.

One's joy in the Lord is not dependent on people, places, or position. God's blessing makes life worth living! As the Psalmist sang, "Weeping may endure for a night, but joy cometh in the morning" (Ps. 30:5).

When Nero was emperor of Rome, there was a group of soldiers known as the Emperor's Wrestlers. These stalwart men were picked from the bravest of the great athletes of the Roman amphitheater. They were the emperor's champions in the games and in the battlefields of the world. Before an athletic contest, the company of men would stand in the arena chanting, "We, the wrestlers, wrestling for thee, O Emperor, to win for thee the victory, and from thee the victor's crown!"

Events led to the necessity of sending the Roman army to Gaul for a military battle. No group of soldiers were more loyal than this band of wrestlers. They had been led by their centurion, Vespasian. However, news reached Nero that many had accepted the Christian faith. The Emperor Nero was determined to exterminate Christians. To be a Christian meant death.

A decree came right from Nero to Vespasian: "If there be any among the soldiers who cling to the faith of the Christian, they must die!"

The news arrived in the middle of winter. The soldiers were camped on the shore of a frozen lake. The hard winter had brought out the best of endurance from the men and had united them more closely. Vespasian was cut to the heart when he read the dispatch from the emperor. However, the first word of a soldier's vocabulary is *duty*.

Vespasian called the soldiers together and asked, "Are there any among you who cling to the Christian faith? If so, step forward!"

Instantly 40 wrestlers stepped forward, saluted, and stood at attention. Vespasian had not expected so many. Yet he announced, "The decree has come from your emperor that any who hold to the faith of the Christian must die! For the sake of your empire, your comrades, your loved ones, renounce this false faith!"

Not one of them stepped back. Vespasian barked, "Until sundown I shall wait for your answer."

At sundown, Vespasian again called the company of men and asked, "Are there any among you who cling to the faith of the Christian? If so, let him step forward!"

Again the 40 wrestlers stepped forward and stood at attention.

Vespasian pleaded with them, but not one man would deny Christ. Finally he said, "The decree of the emperor must be obeyed, but I am not willing that your blood be on your comrades. I am going to order you to march out on the lake of ice, and I shall leave you to the mercy of the elements. However, fires will be kept waiting to welcome anyone who is willing to renounce this false faith."

The 40 wrestlers were stripped to the skin. They turned and marched in columns onto the frozen lake, draped in the darkness of a long winter's night. As they marched in step, the men chanted the old chorus they had used in the arena, but changed one word:

Forty wrestlers, wrestling for Thee, O Christ,
To win for Thee the victory,
And from Thee the victor's crown!

Through the long, cold night hours Vespasian stood by the campfire and waited. All through the darkness he could hear them singing still, though more faint, the wrestlers' song.

As morning was approaching, Vespasian saw one lone figure groping its way toward the campfire—in his suffering he had renounced Christ. But from out of the darkness came the song:

Thirty-nine wrestlers, wrestling for Thee, O Christ,
To win for Thee the victory,
And from Thee the victor's crown!

Vespasian looked at the man coming to the fire, then looked out into the darkness toward the song of faith. Suddenly he jerked off his helmet, dropped his shield, and ran onto the ice, crying aloud:

Forty wrestlers, wrestling for Thee, O Christ,
To win for Thee the victory,
And from Thee the victor's crown!

Children of God, leap for joy! Jesus Christ can satisfy the hungering soul, can bind up the brokenhearted, can strengthen those who will endure to the end!

His kingdom cannot fail:
He rules o'er earth and heaven.
The keys of death and hell
Are to our Jesus given.

Lift up your heart:
Lift up your voice!
Rejoice; again, I say, Rejoice!

—Charles Wesley

Reference Notes

Chapter 1:

1. Ann Landers' column, *Modesto Bee* (Chicago: Publishers-Hall Syndicate).

Chapter 2:

1. William Barclay, *Matthew,* "Daily Study Bible Series" (Philadelphia: The Westminster Press, 1958), 1:83.
2. Kenneth S. Wuest, *The New Testament, an Expanded Translation* (Grand Rapids, Mich.: William B. Eerdmans Publishing Co., 1961), p. 9.
3. E. Stanley Jones, *The Christ of the Mount* (New York: Abingdon Press, 1931), pp. 57-58.

Chapter 3:

1. Charles L. Allen, *God's Psychiatry* (Westwood, N.J.: Fleming H. Revell Co., 1953), p. 133.
2. D. Martyn Lloyd-Jones, *Studies in the Sermon on the Mount* (Grand Rapids, Mich.: William B. Eerdmans Publishing Co., n.d.), 1:53.
3. Myron S. Augsburger, *The Expanded Life* (Nashville: Abingdon Press, 1972), pp. 47-48.
4. Barclay, *Matthew,* p. 90.
5. Peter Marshall, *New and Inspiring Messages* (Kansas City: Hallmark Cards, Inc., 1969), pp. 15-16.

Chapter 4:

1. Allen, *God's Psychiatry,* p. 137.
2. George Arthur Buttrick, ed., *The Interpreter's Bible* (New York: Abingdon Press, 1951), 7:282.
3. Barclay, *Matthew,* p. 91.
4. *Ibid.*

Chapter 5:

1. Augsburger, *Expanded Life,* pp. 57-58.

2. Ian Thomas, *The Mystery of Godliness* (Grand Rapids, Mich.: Zondervan Publishing House, 1970), p. 47.

3. Lloyd-Jones, *Studies in Sermon on the Mount,* p. 78.

4. Barclay, *Matthew,* 1:96.

5. *Ibid.*

6. Lloyd-Jones, *Studies in Sermon on the Mount,* p. 76.

Chapter 6:

1. Clyde M. Narramore, *This Way to Happiness* (Grand Rapids, Mich.: Zondervan Publishing House, 1959), p. 15.

2. Allen, *God's Psychiatry,* pp. 146-47.

3. Jones, *Christ of the Mount,* p. 73.

4. Augsburger, *Expanded Life,* p. 72.

5. John M. Drescher, *Now Is the Time to Love* (Scottsdale, Pa.: Herald Press, 1971), p. 28.

6. Dietrich Bonhoeffer, *The Cost of Discipleship* (New York: The Macmillan Co., 1961), pp. 100-101.

7. Aarlie J. Hull, "A Christian Woman's World," *Herald of Holiness,* March 14, 1973, p. 17.

Chapter 7:

1. Charles W. Koller, *Sermons Preached Without Notes* (Grand Rapids, Mich.: Baker Book House, 1970), p. 20.

2. Lloyd-Jones, *Studies in Sermon on the Mount,* p. 111.

3. R. V. G. Tasker, *The Gospel According to St. Matthew* (Grand Rapids, Mich.: William B. Eerdmans Publishing Co., 1961), p. 21.

4. William Barclay, *God's Young Church* (Philadelphia: The Westminster Press, 1970), p. 70.

5. W. E. McCumber, *Preaching Holiness from the Synoptic Gospels* (Kansas City: Beacon Hill Press of Kansas City, 1972), pp. 98-99.

6. Augsburger, *Expanded Life,* p. 81.

7. J. Sidlow Baxter, *A New Call to Holiness* (London: Marshall, Morgan, and Scott, 1968), p. 36.

Chapter 8:

1. William Barclay, *The Beatitudes and the Lord's Prayer for Everyman* (New York: Harper and Row, Publishers, 1968), p. 92.

2. *Ibid.,* p. 86.

3. Gerald Vann, *The Divine Pity* (London: Collins Clear-Type Press, 1959), p. 169.

4. Colleen Townsend Evans, *A New Joy* (Old Tappan, N.J.: Fleming H. Revell Co., 1973), p. 103.

5. *Ibid.*, p. 99.

6. *Ibid.*, p. 98.

7. *Interpreter's Bible,* 7:287.

8. Barclay, *Matthew,* 1:105.

9. *Ibid.*

10. Barclay, *Beatitudes and the Lord's Prayer,* p. 100.

11. F. B. Meyer, *The Sermon on the Mount* (Grand Rapids, Mich.: Baker Book House, 1959), p. 30.

12. Barclay, *Beatitudes and the Lord's Prayer,* p. 96.

13. Augsburger, *Expanded Life,* pp. 94-95.

Chapter 9:

1. Lloyd-Jones, *Studies in Sermon on the Mount,* p. 132.

2. Barclay, *Beatitudes and the Lord's Prayer,* p. 117.

3. *Ibid.*

4. Meyer, *Sermon on the Mount,* p. 31.

5. Barclay, *Beatitudes and the Lord's Prayer,* p. 119.

6. Jones, *Christ of the Mount,* p. 78.

7. Clifton J. Allen, ed., *The Broadman Commentary* (Nashville: Broadman Press, 1969), 8:106.

8. Barclay, *Matthew,* 1:112.